Upstyle *your* Furniture

First edition for North America and the Philippines
published in 2015 by Barron's Educational Series, Inc.

Copyright 2015 © RotoVision SA, Sheridan House, 114
Western Road, Hove, East Sussex BN3 1DD, England

All inquiries should be addressed to:
Barron's Educational Series, Inc.
250 Wireless Boulevard
Hauppauge, New York 11788
www.barronseduc.com

Publisher: Mark Searle
Editorial Director: Isheeta Mustafi
Commissioning Editor: Jacqueline Ford
Editor: Natalia Price-Cabrera
Assistant Editor: Tamsin Richardson
Design concept: Lucy Smith
Design and layout: Emma Atkinson
Cover design: Michelle Rowlandson
Illustrator: Hannah Rhodes
Tools photography: Neal Grundy

ISBN: 978-1-4380-0556-0

Library of Congress Control Number: 2014932020

Printed in China

9 8 7 6 5 4 3 2 1

Cover image credits
Front cover (clockwise from top left): Dresser given patina
with antiquing wax by Jessica Bertel Mayhall; Twist leg table
distressed using resist layer by Jessica Bertel Mayhall;
Stenciled pink dresser by Stephanie Jones and blue and white
child's chair by Elizabeth Humphreys Moore; Grey dresser
distressed with resist layers by Stephanie Jones; Stained and
varnished swan chair by Stephanie Jones.

Back cover (from left to right): Detail of a painted and
distressed writing desk trimmed in gold leaf with gilt wax on
the pulls by Elizabeth Humphreys Moore; Ombré dresser by
Stephanie Jones; Green chest with patina by Jessica Bertel
Mayhall.

All pieces by me & mrs jones. Photographs by
Stephanie Jones.

Opposite: Bird and branch hand-painted dresser by Rachel
Pereira of Shades of Blue Interiors.

Upstyle *your* Furniture

Techniques and Creative Inspiration to Style Your Home

STEPHANIE JONES

BARRON'S

Contents

SECTION THREE
Resources

Above: Hand-painted ombré tables by Emily Skrehot & Philip Montanus of Uptown Heirloom Company.

Introduction

Are you ready to hit the "refresh" button on your space? On the following pages you'll find instruction and inspiration to do just that. By pulling together just a few readily available materials and shopping your aunt's attic, a local tag sale or thrift store, or your own home, you'll be all set to upstyle your furniture and accessories.

Before you begin a project, it's important to do a little research into what you like most. Take a look around your home. What works? What pleases you? What needs a lift? As you leaf through magazines, books, and catalogs—and "pin" images online—are there some common threads that run through what appeals to you? Pay attention to those elements that catch your eye over and over. Tear or print some images out and create a mood board. Include paint chips and fabric swatches, and develop a direction for your work.

Now, consider what's available. Are there pieces you already have that just need a redo, or is it time to go shopping? Check yard sales, thrift stores, church rummage sales, and online markets for things waiting to be rescued. Take a moment to evaluate each potential piece to make sure it is worth your time and effort. Does it have a little style, nice lines, a special detail? Is it well constructed? If there is damage, is it repairable, or could the issue be worked into your scheme with the right decorative treatment? Furniture does not have to be solid wood to be worthy, but it does make sense to choose something sturdy. Use the charts beginning on page 30 to help plan your work.

Once you've decided on a direction, pull together the tools and materials you'll need, and sort out what kind of preparation needs to be done. Any major repairs should be accomplished first. Flip to page 42 to help decide if your piece needs to have the existing finish stripped off, or perhaps just sanded lightly and cleaned. Your choice of paint techniques comes next, followed by a finish. Does the piece need another layer or two? Beginning on page 102 you'll find lots of ways to create pattern, texture, and interest. Finally, if there are fabric elements to your furniture, jump to page 124 to find ideas on how to embellish upholstery.

At the end of each section, you'll find a case study or two written by a fellow DIYer that is an example of a great project and inspiration to spur you on.

Don't forget to take photos of your piece at the start and during the process— it will be fun (and gratifying) to look back at the "before" once you have the fabulous "after." Now, it's time to jump in!

Opposite: Striped chest of drawers by
Rachel Pereira of Shades of Blue.

SECTION ONE

The Basics

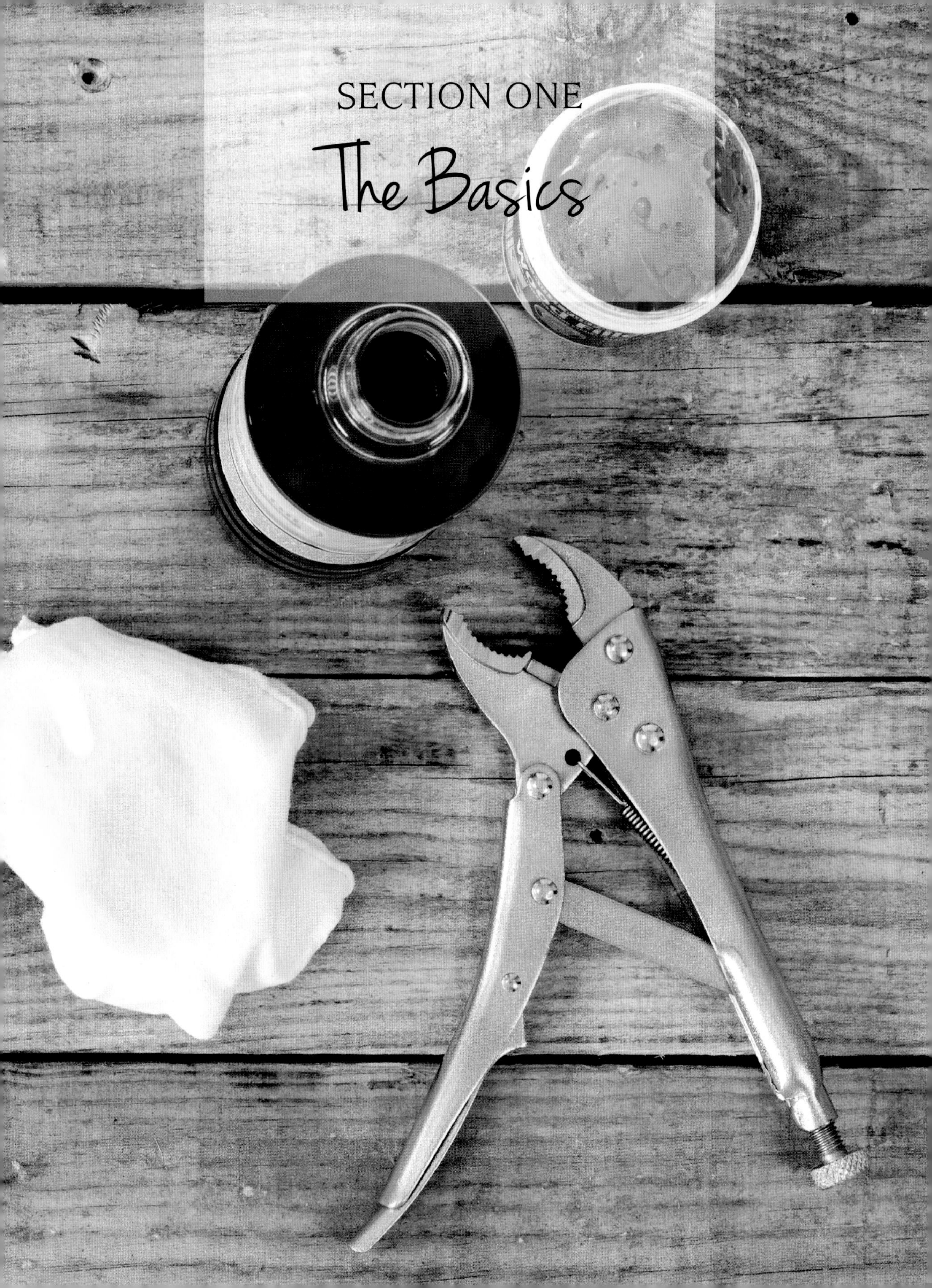

CHAPTER 1
Tools and Materials

Overview

It should go without saying that having the right tools helps any job go smoothly. While you don't need to go and spend a fortune at hardware and art supply stores, or buy everything on the lists that follow, do double check to make sure you have what you need before you start. Each tutorial has a supply list so that it's all mapped out for you. Some tools do double duty, and some materials may already be in your kitchen, closet, or garage. There are some things that are worth the investment: a good metal tape measure, a T-square, and a laser level are all things that will come in handy sooner or later—when it comes time to hang pictures on the wall or square off some flooring, those tools are indispensable.

As far as primers and paints, this is a category that proves the old adage true: you really do get what you pay for. Your finishes will only be as durable as the weakest layer, so don't skimp on a quality primer or shellac if your project requires one. Better quality paints cover in fewer coats and have a nicer feel. The same holds true for waxes and varnishes. Quality really does matter! Better waxes such as beeswax and carnauba contain more good stuff, are soft and easy to apply, and last a long time. Higher quality varnishes and polyurethanes have enough open time so that brushstrokes level out. Your finishes will be all the better for having used the right materials.

Finally, a note about brushes: invest in one or two nice ones, instead of the bag full of throwaways that may seem tempting in the paint aisle at the store. Pick a brush that feels good in your hand and is the right size for the project. Consider the size and shape of a piece, and choose accordingly. In general, brushes made for trim or sash work are well suited for furniture projects, too.

Previous page and opposite: Photographs by Neal Grundy.

Measuring and marking tools

As the saying goes, "measure twice, cut once." This will mean more when using fabrics and trims on the techniques in Section Two, but is something to keep in mind with some paint techniques as well.

You'll need to measure carefully when mixing milk paint, glazes, and color washes, and in creating an ombré color study. Cutting stencils and adding patterns may also require a little math and measuring, but never fear! With some very basic tools (and sometimes by simply trusting your eye), you'll do just fine.

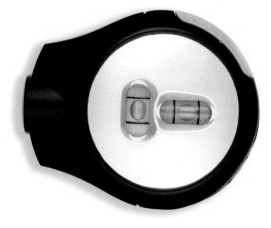

LASER LEVEL
A battery-powered level that allows you to throw a perfectly level beam either horizontally or vertically. The best models have a suction-base that will stay in place while you tape lines and ensure everything's straight.

TAPE MEASURES
A metal tape measure is best for painting projects, while a fabric tape measure is ideal for upholstery and sewing techniques.

SMALL RULER

An 8- or 12-in (20 to 30 cm) straightedge, either plastic or metal.

T-SQUARE

This draftsman's tool makes perfectly sharp corners and ensures straight lines. Great for marking off lines to be cut or embellished on furniture, and for cutting stencils.

PENCILS, ERASER, AND A SHARPENER

Indispensable for marking. Make sure to have an art gum eraser on hand for removing the marks on delicate surfaces.

Measuring and marking tools continued

PERMANENT FELT-TIP MARKER
A fine or medium point. Ideal for making a durable mark on lumber, furniture, and fabrics.

CHALK PENCIL
The ones made for sewing create a finer line than regular chalk and are just the thing for marking fabrics and trims, as well as for chalkboard art.

MEASURING SPOONS
Measuring spoons (typically used for baking), which can be set aside for painting projects are perfect, from a half teaspoon to a tablespoon.

MEASURING CUPS

Ideally, have inexpensive measuring cups that can be washed and reused just for your painting projects in a range of sizes.

PLUMB LINE

Used for vertical marking. Tie a bolt to some twine, tape the other end of the twine to the highest point on your surface, and let gravity find a straight line.

BLACKBOARD CHALK

Very useful for marking on dark surfaces, as well as to use on your painted chalkboard projects!

Primers

Most often, paint needs a foundation coat underneath. Primers have special properties that seal, bond, and provide a surface that paint can hold on to. Don't skip it. Whatever the project, your results will be so much better with it, and not priming when you should have won't save the time or effort you might hope for.

If you're painting a piece that has been previously coated—whether with paint, varnish, polyurethane or another top coat—you'll generally need to prime to get the surface ready for paint.

There are exceptions—some newer paints on the market either do not require priming or have the properties of a primer "built in" to the paint. Once you've primed, you're ready for the really fun part—color.

RUST-BLOCKING PRIMER
For use on oxidized metal. Without a rust blocker, rust will show through your final coats of paint.

SANDING SEALER
If your project piece is oak, the very open grain and aggressive tannins may affect the outcome—enter sanding sealer! Brushing it on and sanding it back will help fill in the grain and seal the tannins in.

SUPER-BONDING PRIMER
These newer, specially formulated primers are meant to adhere to extra-slick, shiny surfaces that used to be considered unsuitable for painting. Apply in a thin, even coat, and allow it to dry for several hours before painting. The primer will feel dry to the touch much sooner, but don't be tempted to rush it—a thorough dry is key to its magic bond.

WATER-BASED PRIMER

An all-purpose base coat for many surfaces. It cleans up with soap and water, and dries quickly so that you can get on with your project. Many latex primers can be used indoors or out.

SHELLAC-BASED PRIMER

If you are painting a piece that has wood stain that might seep through paint (oak and mahogany are notorious for this, as is reproduction furniture stained in cherry and rosewood), a shellac-based primer will seal in those pesky tannins and stains.

ENAMEL UNDERCOAT

Enamel underbodies are made especially to give the smoothest possible finish for oil-based enamels and to block the solvents in those paints from pulling up old finishes. If you're working with an alkyd high-gloss paint, an undercoat like this is a must.

Paints, glazes, and top coats

Now we're getting to the good part where the transformations really happen—paint and topcoats! The number of different paints available for DIY purposes now can be overwhelming, so let's concentrate on the ones that are best for the projects you may have in mind. Quart (0.9l) cans are usually sufficient for furniture projects.

The term **"water-based"** covers a wide range of different paint formulations and is a category that has seen a revolution of sorts in recent years. Water-based paints include—but are not limited to—latex and acrylic. These paints contain resins or polymers that grab on and form a coating. Water-soluble milk paints have casein, or milk protein, as their binder, and are more breathable and porous. Other clay, lime, and mineral-based paints are water-based and porous as well, and need to be sealed for protection. Water-borne paints are generally more earth-friendly, dry much more quickly than oil-based paints, and clean up with soap and water.

Oil- or solvent-based paints are different. They use a natural or synthetic (alkyd) solvent as their base. They are slower to dry, which allows brushstrokes to float out, giving a smoother finish. They are also traditionally thought to be more durable, though advances in paint production have borne extremely durable latex and acrylic coatings. Oil-based paints release volatile organic compounds, or VOCs, into the air as they dry, which are not good for the environment. Brushes and work surfaces must be cleaned with solvents and great care.

Both types of paint are available in different sheen levels, from flat or matte to glossy. The glossier the paint, the harder and more durable it is. Flat paints are easier to sand and distress, and so are better suited to vintage or farmhouse looks. Mid-sheen finishes (satin or semi-gloss) take a glaze much more easily—keep this in mind when deciding on the best paint for your project.

Small bottles of acrylic **craft paint** are widely available and come in handy for smaller projects, stenciling, and for embellishments on bigger pieces.

Stains are made specifically to tone or change the colors of bare wood. They also come in water-based or solvent-based formulations, and are applied with a brush or pad, and then wiped back. You can use stain as an antiquing medium, especially the pretty walnut shades of brown.

A **glaze** is simply a translucent, tintable medium that allows you to add a sheer layer of color over paint. Glazes also come in water-based or oil-based formulations, and for proper adhesion it's best to keep to one or the other—water-based glaze over water-based paint, and vice-versa, though you can use oil-based glaze over water-based paint without any problem. Glazes are most often used to antique or soften a painted finish, giving a patina of age, but they may be tinted to just about any color for many different looks.

Glazes are applied in two different ways: additive and subtractive. In an additive method, the glaze is applied exactly where and how you want it to be. With subtractive techniques, the glaze is put on more thickly, and then manipulated and wiped off to leave it just where you would like.

While no hand-crafted finish is ever bullet-proof, **enamel paints** usually dry with a durable finish that does not need a top coat. When using other paints or stains, you may want to add some protection to your project in one of many ways. **Top coats** are exactly that—a coating that goes on top of paint and/or glaze to protect the finish and (if desired) change the sheen level. They too are made in both water-based and oil-based formulations.

Clear top coats are generally called polyurethane or varnish, though some brands use both terms together so it can get confusing! Keep in mind that water-borne polyurethanes dry very quickly, and so brushstrokes will show. They tend to stay clear over time.

Oil-based varnishes or polys, on the other hand, dry more slowly, allowing brushstrokes to level out. They come out of the can with an amber tone, and continue to yellow as they age, which will affect the lighter colors in your finishes.

Hempseed oil and **tung oil** are protective, natural products that are absorbed by wood and flat or porous paints (such as milk paint). They leave behind a low-sheen protective finish that in some cases is food-safe (check the label though) and may be used outdoors (specifically tung oil). Long favored by woodworkers, oils are finding new fans because they are so easy to use and environmentally friendly.

Waxes are widely available in soft and paste forms, with and without pigment. For furniture projects, soft waxes are much easier to work with, and just as durable once they are buffed and cured. Pigmented waxes are available in a wide range of colors, from brown or gray antiquing formulas to white (or liming) waxes, which give a cerused or bleached, faded look.

All waxes contain a petroleum-based solvent to make them workable. Once they are applied and buffed, the solvent evaporates, leaving only the protective coating of wax. Try different brands to find what suits you best—some waxes offer more shine and protection, while some are more matte but less resistant to spills and spots. Some "clear" waxes have an amber or pinkish tone to them in the can, which may affect the paint colors on your project.

Right: Photograph by Neal Grundy.

Paints, glazes, and top coats continued

WAX
You can buy wax in either soft or paste form. It's generally best used at room temperature.

STAINS
Stains are designed to tone or change the colors of bare wood. You can get them in a range of colors, from lighter oak shades to rich, deep mahogany, and cherry.

ENAMEL PAINTS AND TOP COATS
Enamel paints generally provide a strong final finish for your project piece. If using other paints, you'll want to finish with a top coat to protect the surface from damage and marks.

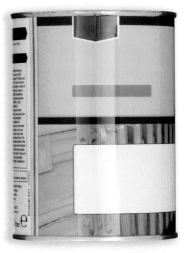

WATER-BASED PAINTS
These paints contain resins or polymers that grab on and form a coating.

ACRYLIC CRAFT PAINT
You can normally buy this in a range of colors and often in small bottles, which is really helpful if you're unsure about a color or only need a small amount (for example, for stenciling).

HEMPSEED OIL OR TUNG OIL
These oils are great not only for protecting wood surfaces but also for making them water resistant.

GLAZE
A translucent, tintable medium that allows you to add a sheer layer of color over a paint finish.

OIL- OR SOLVENT-BASED PAINTS
Oil-based paints are much slower drying, but can create lovely smooth finishes.

Brushes and applicators

Having the right tools on hand makes a project run much more smoothly. When upstyling your furniture with paint, using the correct brush for the technique is key—though often what makes an applicator the "right" one depends on what is most comfortable for you to work with.

Invest in a well-made brush, and you won't be sorry—unless you don't clean and store it properly! With brushes, quality really does matter, and any money you might save on the front end is lost in the time you spend picking loose bristles out of wet paint. The comfort of the handle, the strength of the ferrule and glue that hold the bristles in place, and the quality and density of the bristles themselves are all worth the price.

As a general rule, choose the size of brush based on the surface you're painting: a chair with narrow spindles will call for a ½-in (1.25 cm) sash-style (angled) brush, while a large armoire needs a 3- or 4-in (7.5–10 cm) brush to get the job done quickly. Pick up a brush that's too large or too small, and you'll risk your sanity trying to spread the paint well.

One other factor to keep in mind: your desired finish. A synthetic-bristle brush will put the paint on more smoothly. Natural boar's (or "China") bristles allow you to put more texture into the paint. Choose wisely, and get ready to paint!

FELT OR FABRIC PAD
This or even a folded T-shirt piece is sometimes all you need to put on a thin coat of shellac, wax, or paint, and to wipe back a color wash or glaze.

CHINA, NATURAL, OR BOAR'S BRISTLE BRUSHES
Range from small to large. For furniture projects, a better quality 2- or 3-in (5–7.5 cm) brush is usually just right, though you may need to go larger or smaller, depending on the piece.

HOT-DOG ROLLER

Indispensable for putting paint on quickly and evenly when you're working with large flat surfaces, such as the back of a bookshelf or cupboard, or an armoire. They're also a terrific and quick way to stencil a large area, like a floor. Rollers sized for trim are perfect: 4 in (10 cm).

FOAM BRUSHES

From the craft or hobby department, these are perfect for spreading glues and decoupage media smoothly.

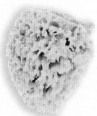

ARTISTS' BRUSHES

Use these smaller brushes (in synthetic or natural bristles) for adding details and doing touch-ups.

SEA WOOL SPONGES

Handy for applying paint and gilding size for special finishes.

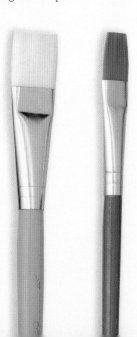

STENCILING BRUSHES

Ranging in size from ¼-in mini-stencilers (0.6 cm) to 6-in (15 cm) block stipplers, a stencil brush has a flat head with bouncy, medium-firm natural bristles, so that paint can be pounced ("stippled") into the pattern.

Other useful tools

Depending on the project you're tackling, there are some other helpful tools and materials to have on hand—some may even be things you already have.

STEEL WOOL
Another versatile abrasive for preparing and finishing your various projects.

SANDPAPER
In varying grits from 120 to 400, this is used to prepare your surfaces and smoothing between coats of paint.

CLAMP LAMPS
Handy for lighting your project area.

A SMALL BOX
For holding hardware and finials when painting (see page 94).

24

A HAMMER

This tool, along with a countersink, finishing nails, and small tacks will be indispensable for small repairs.

DROP CLOTHS

Canvas ones are best, and can be reused over and over. In a pinch, flattened boxes or a shower curtain liner can be used to protect your work area.

A TACK CLOTH

To clean sanding dust before coating.

ZIP-CLOSE PLASTIC BAGS

For sorting hardware on bigger pieces. Label them with a permanent marker.

ABRASIVE CLEANING PADS

These (or abrasive sponges) are used for cleaning pieces and can be used for distressing paint.

Other useful tools continued

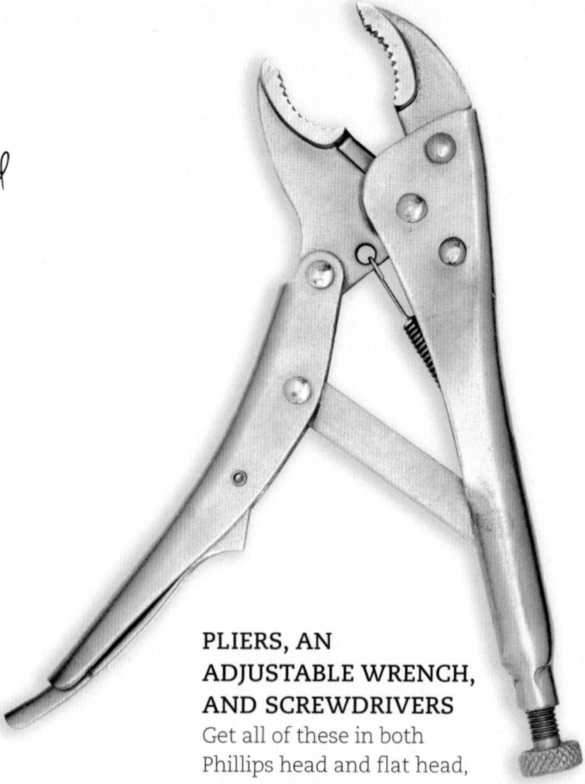

**A CORDLESS
SCREWDRIVER/DRILL**
You'll need this and a set
of bits when it's time to
reassemble things!

**PLIERS, AN
ADJUSTABLE WRENCH,
AND SCREWDRIVERS**
Get all of these in both
Phillips head and flat head,
as sometimes it takes the
lot to remove old hardware
from furniture.

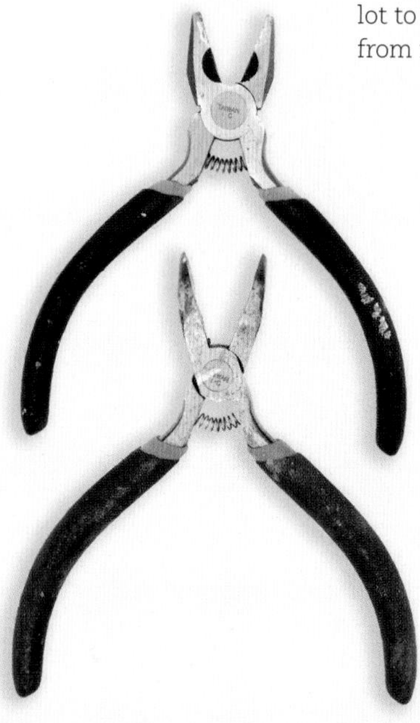

**LOW-TACK
PAINTERS' TAPE**
Used to create clean lines
and edges, and to protect
areas not to be painted.

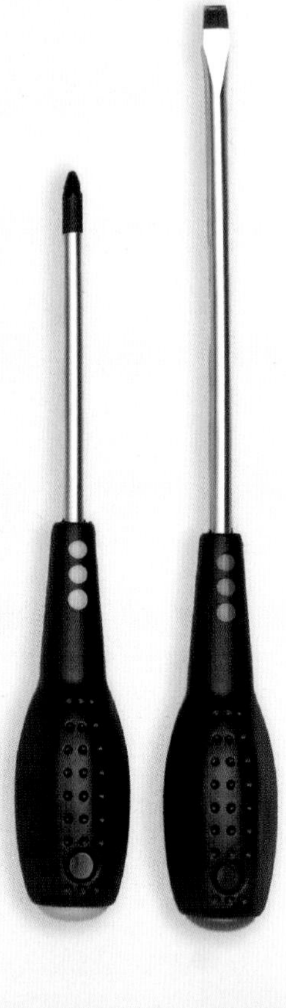

MAKESHIFT CLOTHS

Use old T-shirts and sheets for waxing, shellacking, staining, and polishing.

SUPER-BONDING WOOD GLUE

Used for making all sorts of simple repairs.

CLAMPS

Used in conjunction with wood glue to make repairs. Clamps will hold everything securely in place for the length of the drying time.

MIXING POTS

Remember to save sour cream and cream cheese tubs and plastic take-out spoons for mixing paints and glazes.

WOOD FILLER AND A SMALL PUTTY KNIFE

Used for applying the filler smoothly.

CHAPTER 2

Understanding Surfaces

Overview

So, what are you painting? Most of the time, the answer is obvious: glass, fabric, and metal are all easy to identify. Plastic, laminates, and wood might need a little closer examination, though, since one may resemble another. If wood has a slick, shiny surface, it can be difficult to tell whether or not it's a laminate. Plastic or resin pieces can also fool the eye.

If you're at a flea market or tag sale, ask the vendor if you might take the piece outside into better light for a thorough inspection. Trying to examine something in a dimly lit barn or garage is impossible, and it's easy to miss some major flaws or damage. Give tables and chairs a good wobble test to see if they have too much tell-tale "shimmy," as loose joints can be time-consuming to repair. Sometimes, just tapping the surface of a piece will give obvious clues as to its construction. When in doubt, sanding down just a bit through an existing top coat will often reveal the material. Sometimes you'll need to explore a little further, and remove a screw or look inside a drawer for more information.

Often, you'll find a piece perfect for a redo that may be a hybrid mix. Since one part may require a different step or two, it's important to know your surfaces. Once the piece is finished in a consistent way, though, no one will ever know that it is a mish-mash of materials. Base your decision on whether or not to redo a piece on its stability or fix-ability, its style and lines, and its practicality for your space. Whatever the piece, you'll find clues on the following pages as to the best approach to take when refreshing materials. Refer to the chart that follows for pointers on how to prepare, finish, and care for any of the surfaces you'll be encountering on your upstyling adventure.

Opposite: Hand-painted dresser by Rachel Pereira of Shades of Blue.

Surface characteristics

| WOOD | PREPARATION | WORKING WITH |

WOOD

PREPARATION

Bare, unfinished, or stripped:

- Use wood putty to fill holes, gouges, gaps, and knots.
- Seal stubborn knots or sappy areas with clear shellac. Wipe on with a rag folded into a pad—two or three thin coats. Shellac dries quickly and is non-toxic once it's dry.
- Oak, yellow pine, and mahogany are notorious for their aggressive tannins that will "bloom" through a painted finish. Clear shellac or a shellac-based primer will seal in old stains and tannins, too.

Waxed, sealed, or previously painted:

- Waxed surfaces need to be cleaned thoroughly with mineral spirits to dissolve and remove old wax. Wipe down with shop towels dampened with solvent, turning frequently to a clean side as the wax dissolves. Wash residual solvent away with a mild soap, and rinse and dry completely.
- Wood that is sealed with varnish, polyurethane, or old paint will need a good scuff-sanding with 120- and then 220-grit sandpaper. Remove all sanding dust with a vacuum and tack cloth.
- Really grainy woods like oak can be filled in and smoothed out with a shellac-based sanding sealer.
- If the existing paint color can't be incorporated into or covered by your desired finish, you'll need to strip the old paint before proceeding.
- Fill holes and gaps with wood putty or caulk.

WORKING WITH

- Water-based primers will raise the grain in some woods, so sand them smooth after priming, or leave as they are for a more primitive, rustic look.
- Use clear shellac instead of primer if you'll be doing any distressing, since rubbing back the paint will reveal the white undercoat and not the wood.
- Strong stains such as oak and mahogany can bloom through old varnish and other top coats, especially if they've been sanded. Clear shellac or a shellac-based primer is the best for sealing those in. Wipe on two or three thin coats with a pad made from an old T-shirt.
- Slick factory-type finishes on wood will need an especially enthusiastic sanding, followed by dust removal, a bonding primer, and another light sanding. Start with 120-grit and finish with 220- or 400-grit.

FABRIC

- Pre-shrink any fabrics that you'll want to wash later, such as pillow cases.
- Wash and dry natural-fiber fabrics (like canvas drop cloths and burlap) to remove the sizing and make them ready to accept paint. A cup of white vinegar in the wash load with your regular detergent should do the job.
- Press fabrics smooth before measuring and cutting.

- Some fabrics fray easily, so have some fray check liquid on hand, or bind those pieces with a zig zag stitch on the sewing machine.
- Lighter, thinner fabrics work best on more delicate pieces of furniture, while heavier, bulkier fabrics can go on larger or more simply-lined furniture.
- When choosing a fabric for a dyeing project, go with natural fibers: they will accept pigment much more readily and evenly.

IDEAL TREATMENTS

- Bare wood is an ideal canvas for paint—the sky's the limit! Milk paints are perfect on wood. You can thin them down to use as a stain, or use full-strength for more opaque color.
- Over paint, use a softly contrasting glaze for a traditional look.
- If the wood has pretty color already, seal and enhance it with a tinted wax.
- For beautifully grained woods, use stain and then a top coat for a traditional finish, and combine with painted areas for a more eclectic, modern take.
- Pull out all the stops with wood—here is your chance to try anything. Paint, stencil, decoupage, glaze—let the style of the piece speak to you.
- On paneling or well-grained wood, a soft wash or glaze is a beautiful, subtle effect.
- Stencil or add a graphic pattern with paint using the stained wood as the background.

CARE

- Dust with a soft cloth.
- Painted, sealed surfaces may be cleaned with a damp microfiber cloth and mild soap diluted with water.
- Depending on use, waxed pieces may need an occasional touch-up coat, so use fine steel wool or a nubby cloth and just a little bit of wax to clean, remove rings, and freshen those surfaces up.
- Clean sealed pieces by dusting with a soft rag or wiping gently with a damp microfiber cloth. Mild soap may be used for heavier dirt or spills.

- Machine or hand embroidery, appliqué, and patchwork are all waiting for their chance here!
- Block print or stencil a pattern, from simple to ornate. Spray low-tack adhesive on your work surface to keep the fabric steady as you go.
- Use pre-made rubber stamps (or cut a linoleum block) to create an allover pattern or an interesting border.

- Depending on the fabric and the project, you may want to apply a stain-resistant finish.
- Vacuum regularly with a brush attachment to remove dust and pet hair, especially from upholstered pieces and curtains.
- Follow the manufacturer's instructions for your chosen fabric—some can be machine washed, while other fabrics may need just a spot cleaning with a damp cloth and mild soap, or only a dry-cleaning.

	PREPARATION	WORKING WITH
METAL	• Metal must be squeaky clean and rust-free to accept paint. Commercial rust removers may be very harsh and acidic, so try lemon juice or a baking soda and water paste with fine steel wool for a gentler way to combat mild rust. • Remove any dust or oily residue before painting, using a grease-cutting cleaner, and rinsing carefully.	• Seal metal surfaces with a rust-inhibiting primer before painting—unless a rustic, oxidized look is what you're after, such as with zinc or iron. • Items made of lacquered brass can be painted after removing the lacquer, using a deglosser and acetone. • Read labels—there are a number of different metal paints and primers on the market, so be sure to use the one that's right for the amount of rust and type of metal you're working with. • Use a paint that is made especially for use with metal in high-heat situations when working with fireplace screens and tools and the like.
GLASS	• Glass can be cleaned with ammonia and water, vinegar, or denatured alcohol. • Remove dried paint with a straightedge razor or scraper. • Stickers or other residue will need a solvent to lift them.	• Some paints may require a sealer to be used on glass. Oil-based paint or a high-bonding acrylic paint work well. • Translucent paints can be used for a stained-glass appearance. • If you're going for a milk-glass look, keep in mind that some glass has a greenish cast. You'll need a very warm white to counteract the cool tone of the glass.
PLASTIC	• Plastic can be very tricky to paint, since it's non-absorbent and made to resist dirt and stand up to wear. Make sure it is squeaky clean before beginning by scrubbing with warm water and a grease-cutting soap, and then rinse thoroughly. • Scuff shiny plastic surfaces with 220-grit sandpaper.	• Use a primer made specifically for plastic, or a bonding primer, for the best adherence. • Allow layers of paint and primer to dry completely between coats for proper bonding. Surfaces may feel dry to the touch sooner, but follow label instructions for complete dry time. • Matte-finish resin pieces will accept paint well when clean and primed.
LAMINATES	• A scuff-sanding with 120- and then 220-grit sandpaper is a must. Laminates are made to resist dirt and stains, and will also resist being painted. • Wash down thoroughly with a degreasing cleaner, rinse completely, and remove all sanding dust before priming.	• Use a bonding primer and allow an overnight dry before painting. • Some laminates (such as melamine and thermofoil) are casings applied over medium-density fiberboard (MDF) or molded wood products and are easy to pop off. If so, sand away any glue residue with fine sandpaper, and then seal the MDF so that it can't absorb water from the paint layers. An oil-based primer or sanding sealer is ideal for this.

IDEAL TREATMENTS	CARE
• Metal surfaces tend to be accent areas, and so are great places to experiment on with color and designs. • Use gilding wax to highlight decorative details. • Apply a glaze or wash to give a softly weathered appearance.	• Painted metal is durable but vulnerable to scratches. Dust gently with a soft cloth. • Take care to protect your skin and eyes when working with rust removers.
• Oil-based or gelatin-based gilding size will allow metal leaf to adhere to create a *verre églomisé* look or a mercury glass effect. • Find spray paints in a mirror finish at hardware stores. Spritz the glass with vinegar and water before applying for a spotty, aged look. • "Frosted" glass can be created with a special spray paint that is available at art supply stores. Stencils or decals (that are then peeled off) add pattern to the effect.	• Clean painted glass with care. Dust gently with a soft cloth.
• Smooth, molded plastic pieces lend themselves perfectly to bright, clean, solid-color finishes. • Plastic items with some texture or interest, such as resin flower urns, can easily be given the appearance of old metal or stone with paint and a wash. Use exterior paints for better durability on outdoor pieces.	• Wash or dust gently. Avoid scratching painted plastic, as finishes will be a little vulnerable until well cured.
• Flat-panel style laminates are perfect candidates for a modern, punchy-colored finish, especially the pieces that have the built-in metal handles along the edge. • Other simple styles make a canvas for more imaginative treatments. • Consider taping off "panels" or a graphic pattern. A grained, faux-bois glaze makes a bold statement as it's definitely not wood!	• Allow the painted layers to cure completely (at least 30 days) before any vigorous cleaning. Gentle wiping with a damp microfiber cloth or dusting with a soft rag is best.

Wood

Lots of the furniture out there waiting for its second act is at least partially made of wood, though "wood" can take many forms: solid woods, veneered woods, and chipboard (or pressed board), as well as other manufactured wood products.

Take a peek inside a drawer and joints of a piece for clues when you're assessing something. Furniture with hand-cut—not machine-perfect—"dovetail" joints holding the drawers together is an indication that you've gotten a truly old piece, one that is almost certainly solid wood and built to last. Dovetailed construction sometimes needs a little strategic gluing, as the wood will have been affected by changes in temperature and humidity over the years, and might not fit together as tightly as when the piece was new.

A lot of information can be gleaned from the back and undersides of furniture, too. Pieces with exposed screws or bolts underneath may not be as finely made, but are definitely easier to repair and also usually worth your efforts. These are often solid wood as well, just of a newer vintage. Look for grain patterns to help identify solid wood.

A common issue when painting wood furniture is that old stains or tannins may bloom through the paint. Mahogany and oak are famous for their aggressive tannins, even through a top coat. Sometimes yellow pine, especially the knots, can be a challenge to cover. The most reliable way to lock in an old stain is to use shellac as a barrier before you paint. Available at hardware and paint stores, clear or white pigmented shellac will seal in knots and tannins. Other things to love about shellac: it dries quickly, is non-toxic when dry, and seals in odors such as mothballs or smoke.

You can usually spot pressed-board pieces by looking at hidden spots like the back or edges of shelves for the telltale mashed-together, chippy look. If undoing a screw results in a shower of splintery dust, you likely have a chipboard or pressed-board piece. Made from shaved or ground wood particles, and then shaped using heat, pressed board is an inexpensive material that has the heft of solid wood, but not the grain or durability.

Decide carefully if you should invest time and energy into redoing a wobbly or damaged chipboard piece, since it may not last in the long run. If there is a stapled-on cardboard back panel or drawer bottom, pause again—something that cheaply made may be one to pass on altogether.

Now let's take a look at veneer. Some people refer to this thin layer of wood or laminate on top of a less expensive material as if it were a terrible thing. In reality, plenty of older veneered pieces are beautifully made and will last forever, since they have a thin "skin" of expensive wood laid over a more humble "body," though still of solid wood. Now that laminates and other inexpensively manufactured materials are used as veneers, the name has taken on a negative connotation. But just because something is veneered does not mean it's not worth saving and working on. Please don't sneer at veneer! (See pages 48–49 for fixing damaged veneer before painting.)

Inlay is similar to veneer, but is used to create a pattern in the wood with its variations in color or tone. You'll often see old inlaid pieces showing off pretty lined details, compass roses, checkerboard patterns, stars, and the like. Of course, you can create the look of inlay on a plain piece by using stains in different tones and a stencil.

When painting over inlay, it's nice to show respect for the piece by picking those details up with contrasting paint colors—often the outline of the inlay shows through. Just follow along, using the original design as your guide.

When you have found a beautifully grained and constructed piece, the best way to retain its value is with a loving restoration using the appropriate stain color and a wax or varnish top coat. Damaged, less than lovely, or awkward hybrid pieces with a combination of materials are fair game for paint, decoupage, and other creative treatments so get experimenting.

Opposite: Bright yellow mid-century side tables by Jessica Bertel Mayhall of me & mrs jones/photograph by Stephanie Jones.

Fabric

When looking around your space for project candidates, fabric might not seem among the most likely, but painting onto fabric with some of the methods in the following pages can give your pieces a fresh new look.

Fabrics made from natural fibers such as cotton and linen are going to be the most successful because those materials will absorb paint the best. If you're not sure, and there is no identifying label, spritz a small area with water to see how it behaves. If it soaks in, you're in luck. If it beads up and runs off, reconsider your plan.

Most water-based paints will work well on fabric with the addition of a fabric medium, available at fabric and craft stores. Some specialty paints will adhere well to fabrics and leather, and can be painted directly on with great results—read a few labels before you make a decision.

Outdoor fabrics (including indoor/outdoor rugs) are difficult to try to paint or dye, since they are made to resist, well, everything. It's better to find another project to work on that will give you a satisfying result.

Metal

Furniture and accessories made of metal are easy to identify and, if in good structural shape, are generally sturdy and worth the effort of refinishing or refreshing. Most metal pieces, though, are styled in such a way that—to be authentic—they need to keep a sort of metallic look, though white, black, and bright colors can all work well on certain pieces, too.

When redoing metal pieces, you'll often run into one of two sorts of challenges—the piece will have a slick finish (either powder coated or lacquered) or will be rusty. Either way, there are lots of possibilities for problem solving. The surface characteristics chart on pages 30–33 will give you specifics, but most often, a thorough cleaning and the use of the correct primer will be all you need.

Brass lamps and chandeliers are plentiful at yard sales and thrift shops, and make great project pieces. Depending on the style and shape, brass can take on the look of weathered zinc, be silver-gilded, or be painted to resemble tole or turned wood, crusty with "old" paint and patina.

Outdoors, metal chairs and tables can be freshened up easily. Once any rust is treated, an exterior-rated paint can give a whole new look. Consider any blooming shrubs or trees in your garden when you choose a hue. Urns can also be treated to a refresh with paint, either in a neutral, background sort of way, or as a bright punch of color.

Glass

Glass may be one of the trickier surfaces to paint. First, the kind of paint you use is really important, since glass is so slick. Also, since most often in furniture projects the reverse side of glass is what gets painted, you're basically working backward! On those pieces, the first layer will be the one that shows most, so it really counts.

Tabletops, china cabinet doors, and enclosed bookcases are all great candidates for a reverse-painted glass technique, but decorative accessories offer lots of possibilities, too. Consider an inexpensive "crystal" chandelier, lamp base, vase, doorknob, drawer pull, or decorative jar. A smaller project is the perfect experiment piece before you move on to bigger things. Paints suitable for glass also work well on ceramics, so keep those sorts of items in mind.

Browse the aisles of your favorite art supply center or hobby shop for the most options on special paints or gilding sizes meant for glass. Some are available in very small quantities, since they're meant for smaller craft projects, but you should be able to get larger sizes by special order for a bigger piece. Spray paints in frosted and mercury glass effects are great options for special looks.

Give some layering onto the reverse side of glass a try as well. A lightly stenciled pattern in a pale color first followed by an imperfect coat of silvery "mirror glass" spray paint, finished with a coat of black or dark gray high-bonding paint behind it will give an old, faded-patterned mercury-glass effect. The tutorial for painting on glass with metallic spray paints on pages 108–109 should give you some other ideas, too.

Plastic

Plastic has wiggled its way into our home décor, especially as small pieces and accessories. Picture frames, lamp bases, smaller tables, and stools are what you'll see most of, along with outdoor furniture and containers.

Firm plastic pieces, such as resin, can usually be painted without issues. Things with more "give" or flexibility tend not to take paint very well, or if they do, it doesn't last. Once the surface flexes, most paints—even high-bonding formulas—will fail to adhere. On hard plastic, resin, or a composite material like fiberglass, almost any type of painted finish is possible if the surface is perfectly clean and has been properly primed.

You'll usually be able to identify a piece as a plastic because of its light weight, or by tapping a fingernail on it to hear that telltale "hollow" sound. There are some very pretty and well-designed resin pieces out there just looking for a redo. Once painted, they can take on the look of something much more substantial and much finer, so be creative!

Inexpensive outdoor urns can easily be done up to resemble old stone. Choose a flat-finish exterior paint in a light neutral color, and use a loose wash of mossy green or brown to "dirty" it up, or a gunmetal gray washed with pale blue to give the appearance of weathered zinc. Resin lamp bases, likewise, will take similar treatments beautifully, done in interior-grade paint. Ornate picture frames can fool the eye with metallic treatments or metal leaf.

Laminates

Laminate is the new kid on the furnishings' block, relatively speaking. Developed in the early 1900s, practical laminate has worked itself into lots of useful places in our homes, and can come close to resembling wood, granite, and other more expensive materials.

The good news is that most laminated surfaces can be painted to change their look completely. Roughing up the material with sandpaper, cleaning away any dust, and using the proper bonding primer or paint are the keys to success.

Wooden tables with faux-wood laminate tops are fairly common, and once painted, no one will ever know that they are a mash-up. Those sorts of pieces can be redone any way you like. Other commonly laminate-covered furniture is more boxy and modern, lending itself well to brighter, punchier treatments.

Part of the laminate family is melamine, which is (like typical laminates) bonded, pressed, or glued onto a base of wood or a manufactured relation, such as particleboard. Melamine is part of a newer generation that actively resists being coated and can be difficult to successfully make over with paint. To identify melamine, look for a dark seam on the back of a door or drawer. Kitchen cabinets and office furniture are likely places to find this material.

Laminate countertops that are used in food prep areas in kitchens are better off left alone. Unless tightly sealed with a strong top coat, it is difficult to keep those surfaces food-safe.

WORKING WITH SURFACES

Most of the tutorials in this book have been created on wooden surfaces, unless otherwise stated. Many of the techniques are transferrable however, and the information supplied in this chapter should equip you with what you need to know if you wish to try one of these techniques on a different surface. For instance, the principles of creating an ombré effect are the same whether you're working on wood, plastic, or fabric; simply refer to the surface characteristics chart to see what materials you might need. Once you've learned the basics of a technique such as stenciling (pages 104-106) you could apply it to fabric or plastic, or even be a bit brave and combine it with other techniques such as spray painting (page 108). To make your furniture entirely unique, don't be afraid to experiment with combining materials within a single piece, and the more you learn about the possibilities, the better!

Opposite: Stenciled tabletop, GAP Interiors/Chris Tubbs.

CHAPTER 3
Before You Begin

Overview

Here comes the part that may test the patience or nerve of the most motivated project warrior—stripping, sanding, priming, and repairing, also known in general as "prep work." Try to find your happy place with this stage as it will soon be done, and then you can get on to the fun part of the transformation process!

It may be tempting to skip some or all of these steps, and most projects won't need a lengthy prep process, but it really is important. If you're going to put the time and effort into a redo, don't you want the best possible result? Thought so!

Stripping often isn't necessary (you'll find ways to evaluate whether or not it needs to be done in the following section), but if a piece needs to have the existing finish removed, there's no getting around it.

Sanding isn't so much hard work as it is messy. A good vacuum with a brush attachment is a huge help in cleaning up. Pay attention to the grit level called for at different stages of a project: paper that is too fine won't get the initial work done, and paper that is too coarse will leave "bite marks" in the final finish.

Think of primer as a key undergarment—you wouldn't leave the house without those items on, so don't let your project pieces go without proper foundation, either. Your painted finish will thank you with its appearance, adherence, and durability.

As far as repairs go, making those before you begin any coatings will be a lot easier than trying to go back later to fix and then touch up. Just get the gluing and clamping over with, and then it's on to the creative and colorful steps of your project!

Opposite: Distressed, painted chest, GAP Interiors/Colin Poole.

Tutorial
Stripping

Stripping the existing finish from a piece of furniture is sometimes necessary for a redo, but not always. How to decide? You'll need to strip if:

- You wish to re-stain the wood.
- The surface is too shiny or slick to allow a new finish to adhere.
- The existing finish is damaged and you need a smooth substrate.
- You want to distress down to bare wood without revealing other layers of paint.

But you won't need to strip if:

- Your desired finish can incorporate what's already there.
- You're using products that will adhere well, such as a bonding primer or paint.

It saves time in the long run to test the finish if it's clear. Varnish is more difficult to remove, but can look very much like shellac and lacquer, which are easier. Determining what you're dealing with involves a simple test: rub a cloth saturated with denatured alcohol on the surface. If the finish dissolves, it's shellac. If nothing happens, test again with lacquer thinner, which will liquefy lacquer, but not shellac. A combination of the two is not uncommon, in which case the solvents will soften, but not remove, the top coat. A 50/50 mixture of solvents will soften and strip this particular finish.

Most surfaces you'll encounter, though, are finished with paint or varnish. Removing these involves a chemical process to dissolve those coatings. Stripping products tend to be harsh and smelly, though there are new soy- and citrus-based stripping liquids available that are more earth (and human) friendly. Still, it's best to work with adequate ventilation and preferably outdoors. Every stripping product is a little different—take a moment to read the label.

YOU WILL NEED

- A drop cloth or flattened boxes to protect your work area
- Solvent-proof gloves to protect your hands
- Stripping solution
- An inexpensive or old throwaway brush
- A putty knife
- Coarse steel wool (#4 grade)
- A wire-bristled brush
- Mineral spirits (or product recommended by the manufacturer for cleaning the furniture after stripping the finish)
- Rags

1. Place your piece of furniture on a drop cloth or flattened boxes to protect your work area from the solvent. Apply the stripping solution with a throwaway brush according to the manufacturer's directions. Allow the product to do its job for the recommended time.

2. Use a putty knife to remove the paint or varnish.

3. Use steel wool or a wire brush to scrape away residue on curved sections, or those that have carving or details where paint and other coatings might hide.

4. Take care to follow any safety precautions on the label. Lay any drop cloths, coverings, brushes, and other materials that might contain oil-based stripping solution out flat to dry, and then dispose of as directed.

5. Most stripping solutions call for a final wipe-down with solvent, but some are "wash-away." Try to work quickly during the wash process since excess moisture can easily damage wood and glue. Follow the label directions closely, and dispose of residue, brushes, and rags correctly.

6. Allow your piece to dry completely while you plan its transformation!

1

2

3

Tutorial
Sanding

Go ahead and say it...ugh! Sanding is a bit of a chore, but it is key to a beautiful, enduring finish. Try thinking of it as "smoothing" instead.

When do you need to sand? The tutorials that follow in Section Two will have specific instructions, but most of the time, trust your judgment. Sanding is advisable:

- When a surface is rough or has imperfections that need removing.
- In between coats of primer, paint, varnish, or polyurethane, especially if the paint or top coat is glossy—light sanding will give the surface a "tooth" for the next coat to hold on to.
- When a finish calls for distressing, which can be done with a gentle touch.

For your projects, it's great to have sanding supplies in several different grits on hand, from 120 to 400, and 600 up to 1,000 for special finishes. Think of sandpaper grades the way you would thread count in sheets: the higher the number, the softer the paper will be.

Sandpaper comes in sheets, on sponges, and on blocks. Blocks and sponges are nice to have for large, flat areas (blocks); rounded, curvy parts; and edges (sponges). Hardware stores carry small, reasonably priced power sanders, but for most furniture projects those aren't necessary. Use whatever is most comfortable for your hand and what suits the size of the piece you're working on.

120-grit is the one to start with for rough surfaces, smoothing out splinters on edges, taking a layer of cracked varnish off, and getting through glue where you have removed veneer.

220-grit will give a smoother finish to any of the surfaces listed above. It's also ideal for sanding between coats of paint, varnish, or polyurethane. 220 is also a good starting grit for distressing—if it's not taking the paint back quite enough, go to a lower number.

400-grit is considered a "finishing paper" for a final smoothing before your last coat. Use 400 to smooth out wood filler, too. Anything more coarse may leave noticeable bite marks in the putty.

YOU WILL NEED

- 120-, 220-, and 400-grit sandpaper in sheets, on sponges, and on blocks depending on the project
- Vacuum cleaner
- Tack cloth

1. Fold the sandpaper sheets in half so that they can be easily torn.

2. Fold each half-sheet into thirds so that no gritty sides rub against each other.

3. The half-sheet folded into thirds fits nicely into your hand. It's best to sand with the grain of the wood, or with the construction of the piece, using linear, smooth strokes. Making small circular motions with sandpaper may leave marks that show through your finish.

1

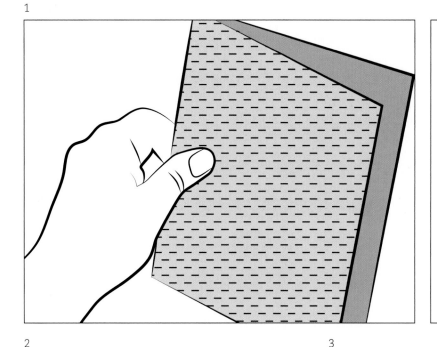

TIPS

Burnishing with 600-grit paper gives a buttery-smooth finish. Milk paint rubbed down with hempseed oil and 600-grit "wet/dry" sandpaper polishes the paint and the oil together, creating a silky feeling and beautiful sheen. Sandpapers from 600–1,000 grit are available at auto supply shops.

Remove sanding dust with a vacuum (the brush attachment is handy) and then a tack cloth, and you're ready for the next step!

2

3

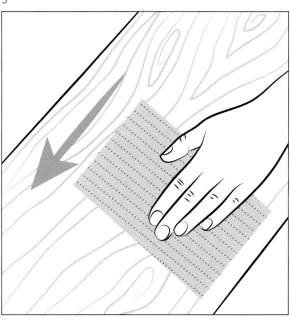

Tutorial
Priming

Priming is a simple but important step on your way to a beautiful furniture transformation. Remember, priming is what gets the surface ready to accept paint. It seals in and covers up imperfections, blocks old stains and odors, and gives the paint something durable to hold on to. Skip priming and you'll likely have to make extra spot touch-ups or apply additional coats of paint.

Determine the correct primer for your project, based on the descriptions on pages 16–17. A synthetic bristle brush (or a foam brush for a small project) will be best, as this coat needs to be smooth. When you're making a big change in color, such as going over dark brown with an off-white paint, two coats of primer will help.

Stir the primer thoroughly before beginning. Some of the "magic" in primers will sink to the bottom while the can sits on the shelf, so make sure to get it all reincorporated. Primers tend to be thin and can be splashy, so don't skimp on covering your work area with canvas drop cloths, flattened boxes, or plastic sheets.

Brush the primer on, taking care not to let it drip or puddle—when it dries, it will be difficult to remove the excess. Avoid over-brushing, especially on slick surfaces—it's easy to accidentally begin to brush away primer that's just begun to dry.

If you see any brown, pink, or orange stain (or knots or marks of any kind) start to "bloom" through the primer, you'll need to seal that surface with either clear shellac or a shellac-based primer, applying two coats to block the stain.

Sand lightly in between coats with 220- or 400-grit paper, and remove all the sanding dust. The brush attachment on a vacuum cleaner, followed by a tack cloth wipe-down is the best way to thoroughly clean any dust away. A tack cloth is a cheesecloth that's pretreated to be slightly sticky. After removing it from the package, unfold it all the way and then lightly bunch it up to wipe, changing to a fresh side of the cloth every few passes.

Once the primer is dry, you're ready for the really gratifying part of your project—color! Make sure you follow label directions for the correct dry times as some primers offer a quick break before re-coating, while others need an overnight dry.

TIP

When loading your brush for priming, painting, or top coating, remember to just dip the very tips of the bristles into the liquid. Overloading a brush causes puddles, splatters, and waste. Dip the tips in, shake gently to lose any excess, and then go to your surface, brushing with the grain of the wood.

YOU WILL NEED

- Primer
- Synthetic bristle brush or disposable foam brush
- Protective drop cloths
- 220- or 400-grit sandpaper
- Vacuum cleaner
- Tack cloth

1. After sanding, use a vacuum with a brush or crevice attachment to remove sanding dust.

2. Follow vacuuming with a wipe down with a tack cloth to make sure you've caught all the dust.

3. Brush primer on, following the grain of the wood.

4. A disposable foam brush is good for priming small projects, especially when using a shellac-based primer, which can be hard to clean.

Tutorial
Repairing

So much furniture, so little time! There are countless pieces out there just waiting to be rescued. Some just need a good scrub-down to be ready for their transformation. However, there are those that need a little bit more. Don't let the thought of minor repairs keep you from choosing a worthy project candidate though.

You don't need an expensive, fully loaded tool kit to be a furniture-saving hero. Here are some of the most common, easy-to-solve problems.

Loose or peeling veneer Use super glue. Those little tubes have long nozzles for a reason! Gently ease the nose of the tube between the veneer and base as far as you can without risking a break, and squirt a bit of glue in. Clamp the pieces together, and wipe away any excess glue that might seep out. If needed, tap a finishing nail in place to reinforce the bonded area. Counter-sink the nail so that it is flush with the surface of the wood. Patch with wood filler where needed, and smooth it with fine sandpaper when it's dry.

1. Use wood glue with a squirt nozzle and a clamp to hold loose bits in place while the glue dries.

2. Gently pull loose veneer away to squeeze glue in.

3. Tap in a small finishing nail or brad to hold the veneer in place.

4. Use a hammer to tap the nail in all the way.

Missing sections of veneer If the veneer layer is missing pieces, secure the edges around the broken area with glue or nails as necessary, and use wood putty to fill in the gaps, spreading it with a putty knife or the edge of a credit card. Smooth it when it's dry with 400-grit sandpaper.

If the veneer is a total wreck—warped from water damage or worse—drastic measures are called for! Dampen a bath towel with water and lay it across the veneered surface. Turn an iron to its hottest setting, and working one spot at a time, let it sit on the damp towel. The resulting steam should loosen the glue that holds the veneer in place, allowing you to carefully pry it off. Once it's removed, using 120-grit sandpaper, smooth away any remaining glue.

Drawer runners Often, a wonky drawer won't close properly because the runner is loose. You may need a flashlight to peek inside and assess the situation. Use a hammer and nail if possible, or super glue at least, to re-secure the piece. A little wax or soap on the runner will get the drawer gliding more smoothly.

On newer furniture, especially cabinets, the metal drawer slides might just want a bit of WD-40 or oil to get them moving well again.

1. Tighten nails or screws that hold drawer runners in place so that they will open and close smoothly.

2. A spritz of spray oil helps metal drawer runners slide like new.

YOU WILL NEED
- Super glue
- Clamps
- Nails
- Sandpaper of various weights
- Wood filler/putty
- Cloth
- Putty knife
- Bath towel
- Iron
- Needle-nose pliers
- Hammer
- Oil/WD-40

Wobbly legs on tables and chairs
Most pieces that you'll find suitable for upstyling have been made recently enough that there are metal screws or bolts holding the legs in place. Using needle-nose pliers, tighten up the joints. A little super glue in the gaps doesn't hurt, either.

1. Use needle-nose pliers to tighten the nuts and bolts that hold wobbly chair or table legs.

Loose or peeling veneer 1

4

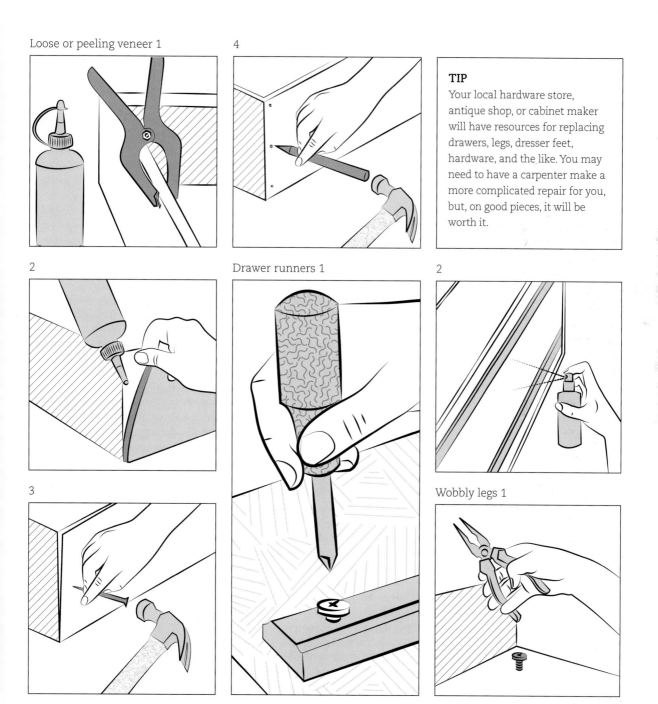

2

Drawer runners 1

2

3

Wobbly legs 1

TIP

Your local hardware store, antique shop, or cabinet maker will have resources for replacing drawers, legs, dresser feet, hardware, and the like. You may need to have a carpenter make a more complicated repair for you, but, on good pieces, it will be worth it.

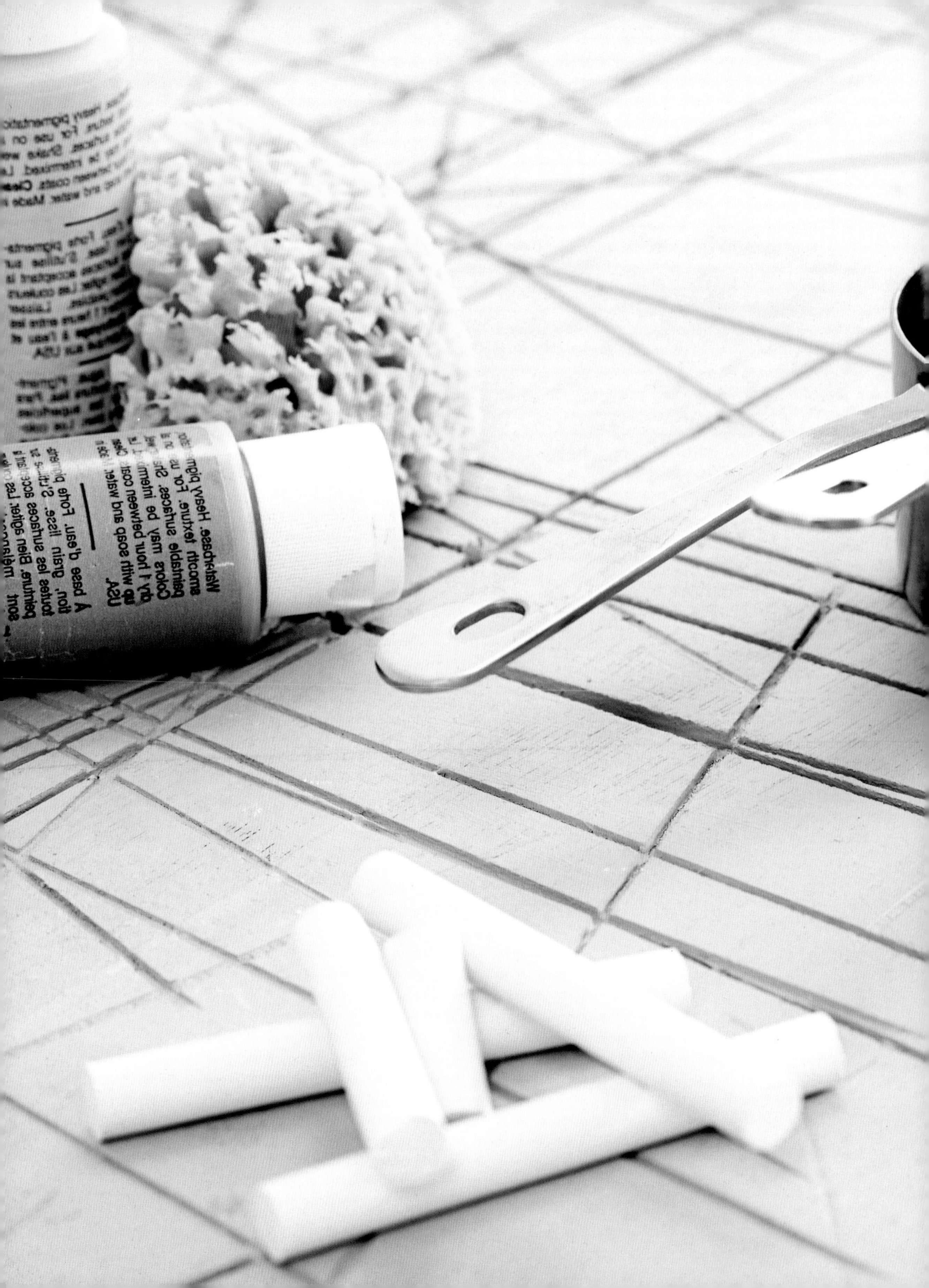

SECTION TWO

Techniques

CHAPTER 4

Paint Techniques

Overview

Over time, paint has been used as a way to elevate and protect humble furnishings, to enhance the very finest pieces, and to express the owner's individuality—so really, nothing has changed! Painting a piece of furniture gives you the opportunity to update, customize, and create something special.

There are a few guidelines to keep in mind when planning a potential painting project:

On larger pieces or utilitarian, work-a-day furniture, keep the color scheme more neutral. A busy, metallic, or colorful finish will call attention to a piece. Make sure it's worthy of the spotlight and that the room it lands in will have enough balance. Softly washed color, gently distressed layers, and maybe a little dry-brushing to highlight the details will suit those pieces. A smaller piece with interesting lines or shape might be ready for its close-up. Consider these for a more knock-out, "look at me" kind of pop using metallic paints, a lacquer look, or metal leaf. A modern, mid-century, or chinoiserie-style project makes a perfect canvas for a bright, high-gloss punch of color or an ombré-style color study.

Primitive, farmhouse, or cottage style furniture is best served with a simpler finish, such as a wash or gentle distressing, while a piece with lots of curves, trim, and details gives you a canvas for a virtuoso sort of treatment using stencils and gilded touches.

Once you know the rules, feel free to break them all! The ways in which you can layer and combine the paint techniques that follow make for endless possibilities. Use these tutorials as a starting place, and let your imagination and creativity have a long leash.

Previous page: Photograph by Neal Grundy.
Opposite: Chalkboard painted tabletop by Melissa Hesseling of Fawn Over Baby Blog.

Tutorial
Color washing

A wash is simply a diluted coat of paint applied to a surface. Washes add a translucent layer of color and are used when:

- The base color needs softening, adjusting, or toning down a little.
- You want layers of color, but distressing with sandpaper might reveal an unappealing surface beneath your finish.
- An aged or patinated effect is desired.

Mixing and applying a wash is a simple process, though large, flat surfaces can be challenging because the wash can begin to dry, creating crusty edges in your finish. A small dresser or nightstand, or a piece that has sections (such as a tabletop with planks) work well. When using a wash on a larger area, an "extender" will help. This is

a water-based product added to the wash that keeps the paint wet longer, allowing for more workable or what is known as "open" time.

Here, we're going to wash one paint layer over another. Choose colors that have enough contrast so that one will show through the other—hues that are too similar will just blend together. Try pale blue over a charcoal color for an oxidized zinc look on a lamp base, or a mossy green wash over a stony gray on concrete urns.

A wash will settle into and enhance any details or carving. Likewise, it will call attention to any imperfections on a surface, so prep accordingly.

YOU WILL NEED

- Water-based paint in two colors (eggshell or satin for your base coat)
- Natural bristle brushes for the paint and the wash, plus a spare "dry" brush
- A small bucket of water
- An empty container to use for mixing the wash
- Soft, lint-free rags
- A spray bottle filled with water
- A top coat of your choice

1. Apply two coats of the base color paint and let them dry thoroughly.

2. Mix a small amount of wash by diluting the second paint color about 40%:60% with water in a separate container, stirring well.

3. Dip a brush into clean water, and shake off the excess. Natural or "China" bristles will absorb and hold a little water, making this step go much more smoothly. Load the damp brush with the wash.

4. Slather it quickly over a section of your surface.

5. With a rag, pat and drag the wash to create the effect you want (see steps 5a and 5b), letting it settle into any nooks and crannies, leaving as much as desired.

6. If needed, spritz the surface with water to keep the wash workable.

7. If the washed areas develop a "dry edge," use a clean, dry brush to stipple and blend sections together, and to soften the places that need it. Allow the wash layer to dry completely, and then apply a top coat for protection.

3

5b

6

4

5a

7

Tutorial
Creating an ombré effect

Ombré means simply "to shade." Using ombré on furniture is a dramatic way to explore the gradations of a color, giving a soft, faded look in colors like pinks and violets, or a modern punch in more saturated tones. Picture the way the hues on a paint chip from the hardware store look, with the deepest color at the bottom, lightened with white as the colors go up. It really can be a very striking effect!

Choosing a piece of furniture that has pre-determined sections—such as a dresser with several drawers—makes creating an ombré color study easy. A bench with horizontal slats or a tall bookcase would also be perfect canvases for a shaded treatment, as would the risers on a staircase.

Spend a minute making a color chart and a plan. If you're painting bookshelves or the like, you may need to tape off sections using painter's tape for a nice, crisp line between shades.

YOU WILL NEED

- Water-based paint in a bright or deep color (your "primary") and in white, in a flat or eggshell finish
- Recycled spoons, tubs, and a measuring cup for mixing
- A piece of watercolor paper (or poster board) for testing colors
- A synthetic bristle brush or two (with an angled end for the inside of bookcases and other tight spaces)
- Painter's tape
- A top coat of your choice (unless you use an enamel-type paint)

1. Decide how many different shades of the "primary" color you'll need, based on the sections or drawers.

2. With a small tub for each shade, create a mixture of the primary plus white for each: 1 spoonful to 1 spoonful, 2-to-1, 3-to-1, and so on. Begin with small dabs of paint and make a note of your ratios.

3. Paint swatches of each shade on the paper, let dry, and adjust any as necessary. Then mix more paint in each shade, using the same ratios, with a small measuring cup. (For a typical dresser, allow around a cup [250 ml] of paint per drawer.)

4. Beginning with a prepped and primed piece, apply two coats of the paint, allowing for drying time in between. First, paint the body in the primary color.

5. Then, starting with the bottom drawer, shelf, or section, apply two coats in the darkest of your shaded mixes, allowing drying time in between. Work your way up, using the next lighter shade for each section. Apply a top coat of your choice to protect the finish.

TIP
Keep in mind that your base color plus white may step into unintended territory—blues, greens, and violets work well for ombré, but some shades of red and orange can go from bold and vibrant to overly sweet very quickly, so keep this in mind.

1

4

2

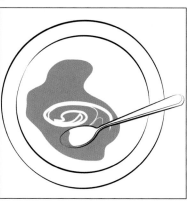

The finished piece

3

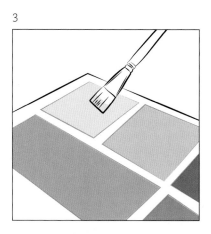

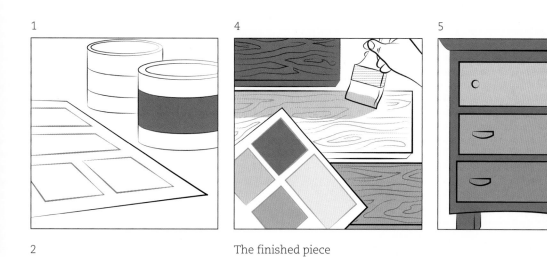

5

Tutorial
Metallic paints

There are some fabulously glam metallic paints available now that are water based and just as simple to use as any other acrylic paint. Gold, silver, copper, bronze, platinum—get rich quick!

Since any sort of gloss magnifies imperfections in a finish, you'll want to make sure that your piece is as smooth as possible. The paint may look like metal, but it is not bulletproof! So, for extra depth and protection, a gloss polyurethane top coat can be added too.

Consider using metallic paints to update lamp bases, frames, and other accessories, or to give a luxe gleam to a desk, nightstand, or cocktail table.

1

YOU WILL NEED

- 220- or 400-grit sandpaper
- A tack cloth
- A synthetic bristle brush
- Water-based metallic paint
- Acrylic top coat in gloss finish

1. Patch any holes or gouges with wood filler, and then sand the surface smooth. Use a tack cloth (unfolded all the way, and then bunched back up) to wipe the surface clean of all sanding dust.

2. Lay the paint on with long, smooth strokes. Avoid over-brushing! Work from a dry area into wet paint, so that you don't over-work the paint you've already applied.

3. When the first coat is dry, smooth the surface lightly with fine sandpaper to give the surface a little "tooth" for the next coat to hold on to (a). Wipe again with the tack cloth, turning and re-bunching it to expose a clean side (b).

4. Brush on a second coat of paint, using the same smooth strokes.

5. When the paint has dried completely, add a top coat to the metallic finish with the high-gloss polyurethane, again sanding lightly between coats and tacking in between coats. Allow to dry thoroughly before placing anything heavy, wet, or sharp on top.

2

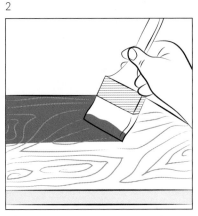

3a

3b

The finished piece

4

5

Tutorial
Metal leaf

Traditional gilding is a delicate process involving fine clay, glue kept at a constant temperature, gloves, and polishing with a stone. Luckily, new products short cut the method, with terrific results. Gilding gives a texture and shine unlike any brush-on product.

Metal leaf comes in its pure form in silver, gold, and copper. It's also available, though, in affordable alloys that provide an authentic look and a lot of wow at a much lower cost. The leaf comes as a "book," each containing 25 small square sheets of the tissue-thin foil.

Size, the special glue that is made for the gilding process, comes in water-based and oil-based formulas. Oil-based is best for slick surfaces such as resin, glass, shiny metal, or alkyd paint. Water-based size works well over most painted surfaces.

Line the edges of a piece with a gilded ribbon, or go all out and cover a chair, nightstand, or dresser for a super glamorous statement.

YOU WILL NEED

- Low-sheen water-based paint in a color to contrast with your choice of metal
- A paintbrush
- Small artist's brushes in various sizes
- Water-based gilding size
- Metal leaf (one book is sufficient for most small projects)
- A soft brush
- A soft cloth
- Shellac, varnish, or wax to seal the surface

1. Paint a base coat onto your primed and prepared piece of furniture, and let it dry completely.

2. Using an artist's brush in a size that suits the area you're working on, apply the gilding size wherever you want the leaf to be. Take care not to let it drip or puddle—a smooth, even coat is key.

3. In just a few minutes, the size will become clear and barely tacky to the touch. Gently float a leaf into place on the size, and brush it softly to help it adhere. Brush away any excess, saving these "skewings" to fill in bare spots later.

4. Repeat until you've covered all of the sized areas.

5. Polish gently with a soft cloth to make sure all of the leaf has adhered, and to remove any leftover bits.

6. Seal with shellac or varnish to protect the gilded surface, or use a tinted wax to antique your gilding, if you like.

1

2

3

4

5

6

TIP

If you're gilding a large area, such as a tabletop or wall, apply the size with a foam roller. Begin with a full sheet of leaf at the center, and work out and around.

The finished piece

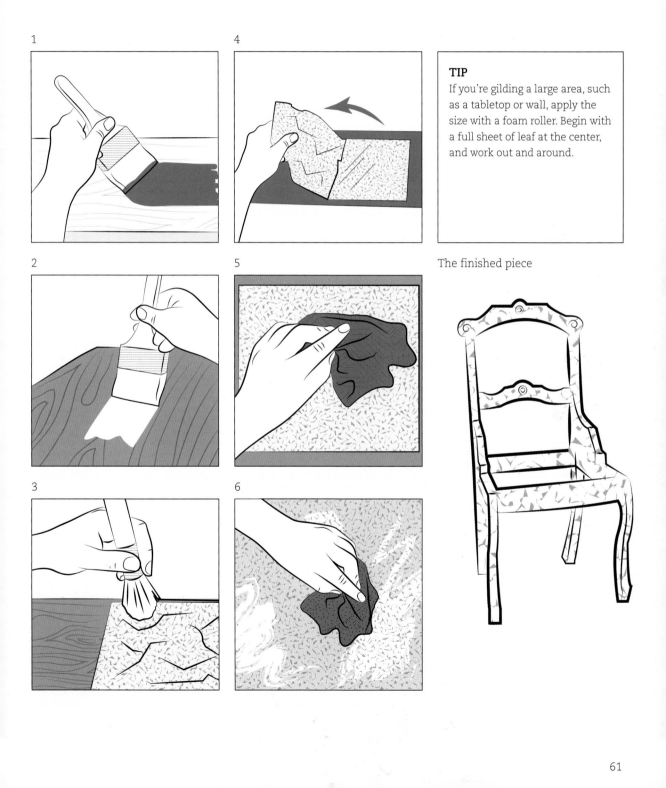

Tutorial
The lacquer look

Do you have a special piece that deserves some wow? Try a rich, glossy shine. A true lacquer requires many layers, rubbed vigorously in between, but a lacquer look for furniture and accessories can be achieved with a glossy paint or top coat. For maximum shine and depth, use oil-based enamel in high gloss or a gloss polyurethane top coat over enamel.

Polyurethanes have an amber tone to them, and so are best over deeper colors. If you're using a light color, choose a top-quality high-gloss enamel instead, to avoid yellowing.

Your results will be gorgeous, but patience and a dust-free, well-ventilated workspace are vital. Shine will magnify any imperfections on a surface, so prep thoroughly beforehand.

YOU WILL NEED

- Clean canvas drop cloths (plastic causes static and dust)
- 220- and 400-grit sandpaper
- Vacuum with brush attachment
- Tack cloths
- An enamel underbody primer
- High-gloss paint or an oil-based enamel paint, and a gloss top coat
- A top-quality paintbrush, specifically for oil paints
- Mineral spirits or paint thinner
- A glass jar for cleaning brushes

1. Stand the piece of furniture on top of the drop cloths. After you've made any repairs necessary, such as filling holes with wood putty, sand the piece perfectly smooth.

2. Remove all sanding dust with a vacuum, and wipe down well with a tack cloth that's been unfolded and bunched up.

3. Shake any sanding dust out of the drop cloths, and vacuum to make sure your work space is dust-free.

4. Apply a smooth, even coat of enamel underbody to the surface. When the primer is dry, sand lightly with 220-grit sandpaper, and remove all the dust again from the piece and your work area.

5. Put on a coat of paint, taking care to keep it nice and even.

6. Brush from an unpainted area back into your "wet edge"—this will keep the paint from getting over-worked. Don't overload your brush, or the paint might "sag" on vertical surfaces. Nice and even is the key!

7. Let the paint dry thoroughly. (In humid climates, this can take up to 36 hours. If you sand too soon, the paint may still be soft and the finish will be damaged.) Sand gently with 400-grit paper and remove all dust completely.

8. Repeat with a second coat of paint. If you're using oil-based enamel, allow the paint to dry, and you're finished! If you're adding a high-gloss top coat, allow a full dry followed by gentle sanding and dust removal, and then careful application of the polyurethane with a clean brush.

9. Clean your brush(es) using the minimum amount of mineral spirits possible, and carefully dispose of the residue according to the directions on the container. Give the paint and top coat plenty of time to dry completely before putting the hardware back on the furniture.

1

5

8

2

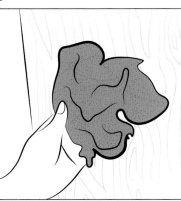

The finished piece

4

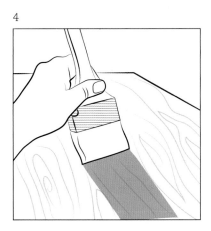

Tutorial
Chalkboard paint

For old-school fun with a piece of furniture, try one of the many new water-based chalkboard paints available. Though any latex paint in a flat finish will work as a surface for chalk art, the paints made specifically for chalkboards will stand up to lots of wiping and erasing.

Consider a desktop, a child's table, a file cabinet, a dresser—the possibilities really are endless. Pop a chalkboard-painted plywood panel into a decorative frame to hang, or paint a panel directly onto a wall or door. Just make sure to have plenty of chalk on hand when inspiration strikes!

2

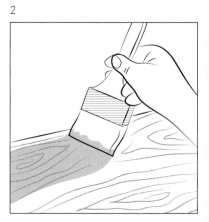

YOU WILL NEED

- 220-grit sandpaper
- Tack cloth or damp cloth
- Latex paint in a color and sheen of your choice
- Synthetic bristle brushes
- Low-tack painter's tape
- Chalkboard paint in a complementary or contrasting color
- A foam or short-nap roller (optional)
- Chalk

1. Prime your prepared piece and allow to dry. Sand lightly, and wipe away all the sanding dust with a damp cloth or a tack cloth.

2. Base-coat the piece with latex paint. After it's completely dry, apply a second coat for full coverage, sanding lightly in between coats.

3. Tape off the area(s) that will become chalkboard—a rectangle in the center of a desk or tabletop, or drawer fronts—wherever you like.

4. Carefully apply two coats of the chalkboard paint within the tape, using a brush or roller, and allowing drying time in between coats.

5. Remove the tape while the second coat of paint is still a little wet, otherwise the paint may lift off together with the tape.

6. Allow the chalkboard paint to cure according to the label. Then, "prime" the paint by rubbing the entire chalkboard surface with white chalk.

7. Wipe it clean and then you're ready to go!

TIP

If you've created some chalk art that you're especially proud of, preserve it by spritzing with hairspray or a spray fixative from the art supply store. The chalk will fade a little while wet, but should brighten up again when dry.

3

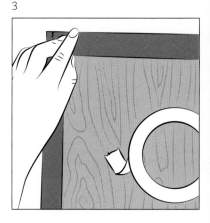

4

5

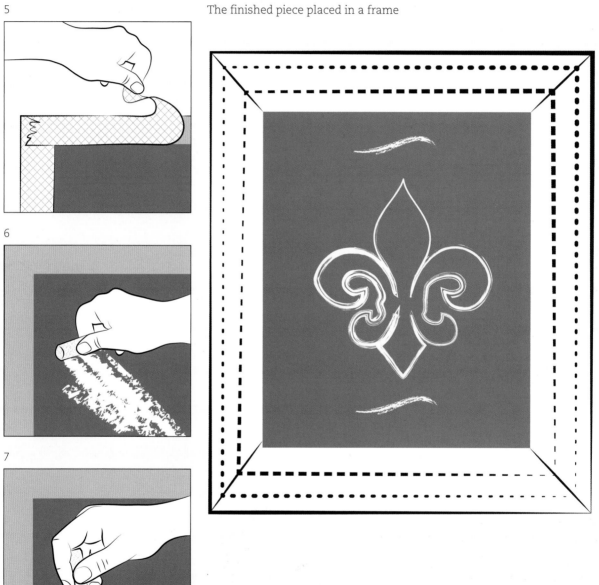

6

7

The finished piece placed in a frame

Tutorial
Faux bois

With the current craze for bringing the outdoors in, faux bois (from the French for "false wood") is a natural fit in almost any decorative mix. Once used to elevate less-expensive woods, the technique of creating wood grain with a glaze looks fresh again in pretty neutrals or in fantasy hues not found in nature. Choose a piece that has flat planes. Carved details and tight spots make graining difficult. However, a Parsons-style table or plain dresser will make great projects.

YOU WILL NEED

- Latex paint in either two contrasting, tone-on-tone, or complementary colors (enough of one color for two coats on your piece, and a small amount—a few tablespoons— of another)
- Paintbrushes for your primer and base coats, as well as a soft-bristled brush for glazing
- 220-grit sandpaper
- Tack cloth or damp cloth
- Latex glazing medium
- Small foam roller and a roller tray
- A rocker grainer tool
- Soft rags
- Top coat of your choice

1. Prepare and prime your piece. Apply two coats of the base color, sanding lightly and wiping away the dust between coats, and allow the paint to dry thoroughly.

2. Mix a glaze with your second color according to the label directions. Generally, it's one part paint to five or six parts glazing medium.

3. Pour the glaze into the roller tray, and coat the roller, allowing it to absorb the glaze for a couple of minutes. Offload excess glaze on the ribbed part of the tray.

4. Roll a thin, even layer of glaze on to one section of your piece at a time—for instance, one drawer front. If your piece has large surface areas, roll the glaze in sections that run the long way, as the grain of the wood would do.

5. Pull the grainer through the wet glaze, rocking it as you go to create a pattern in the glaze. Wipe any glaze from the grainer, and then pull it through again, alongside your first pass.

6. Keep moving along like this, adding another section of glaze as needed. Leave an untouched area of glaze along the edge of a section so that you can blend the next roller-full of glaze into it.

7. As you finish each area, use a soft, dry brush to gently blend any glaze that might need softening, and to catch any drippy or uneven spots along the edges.

8. Allow the glaze to dry completely, and then seal it to protect the finish with a clear top coat.

TIP
Add layers of off-white or pale gray paint dry-brushed over your "grained" surface to give the impression of driftwood or sun-bleached timbers. Dry-brushing will add softness and depth, as well as distracting the eye from any less-than-perfect spots in the glaze.

2

5

6

3

7

4

Tutorial
Dry brushing

A way to build up layers of color with soft brushstrokes, dry brushing adds lots of gorgeous texture to a piece with very little effort. The key is to use very little paint on the brush at a time, and light, feathery brushstrokes.

Dry brushing is a versatile finish for lots of projects, from cabinets and dressers to lamps and baskets. On a simple piece of furniture, it can add softness and interest, creating a driftwood look in neutrals or a rich finish in more saturated colors. It can highlight details on a piece of furniture, so if you have something with interesting carving or trim, give dry brushing a try.

YOU WILL NEED

- Latex paint in a couple or three different colors, a larger amount for your base coats, and smaller amounts of the others
- A good synthetic brush for the primer, and 2 in or 3 in (5 cm or 7.5 cm) chip brushes for each color of paint
- Recycled jar lids from your kitchen
- 3 or 4 paper towels
- A tinted glaze or pigmented wax
- A top coat of your choice (if using glaze)

1. After prepping and priming your piece, apply a coat or two of your base color and let it dry.

2. Pour a couple of spoonfuls of the first accent paint color into one of the lids—you'll just need a little paint at a time.

3. Using a chip brush—the more bristly the better—dip just the tips into the paint.

4. Offload any excess onto a folded paper towel. Now you have a "dry brush."

5. With quick, random strokes, feather the paint on, reloading and then offloading the brush as necessary. You will only cover about 30–40% of the piece with this coat of paint, so a lot of the base color will still be showing. If the piece has a lot of carved areas, stipple paint into those details by pouncing the brush.

6. Repeat the process with the next color and a fresh brush, building up layers. The more random your brushstrokes, the better.

7. Repeat again with a third color, if desired. On this go-round, you might just hit any raised areas with the bristles to highlight those details.

8. If you'd like, tone down the layers with antiquing glaze or pigmented wax. If you've used glaze, you will want to protect the finish with a top coat.

TIP
If you've done a piece in neutral tones, try dry brushing a feathery layer of white, off-white, or pale gray to give the effect of limed or cerused wood.

Tutorial
Distressing with resist layers

An easy way to create a chippy, shabby, farmhouse look is to use "resist layers" to keep paint from adhering well. It may sound counterintuitive, since you're usually working to have the paint stay on a piece, right? So, for this method, skip the primer.

Resists are anything that will prevent the paint from sticking: wax, oil, even petroleum jelly. Chances are that you have plenty of resist agents in your kitchen or bathroom cabinets!

A simple, rustic piece of furniture is perfect for this type of finish, though you can certainly choose something with pretty curves and details. For a truly primitive look, begin with something that's bare wood or stripped, though you can get a great effect by using resists between layers of paint, too.

YOU WILL NEED
- A resist agent or two: paste wax, a taper candle, petroleum jelly (Vaseline™), hempseed oil, nonstick cooking spray
- Latex paint or milk paint in one or two colors
- A paintbrush
- A chip brush
- Sandpaper or coarse steel wool
- Antiquing wax

1. Use your choice of resist agents: rub the side of a candle along edges, stipple Vaseline™ or paste wax on raised details, spritz a little nonstick cooking spray onto the legs of a table or chair—wherever you wish to see the base layer come through. Aim for 20–30% coverage with your resists, though more or less is certainly fine.

2. Brush on a generous coat of paint and allow to dry. Don't overwork the paint—your brush may pick up some of the oil or wax and spread it around. Be free and loose with your brush strokes. Remember you're after a rustic finish!

3. Once the paint is dry, you'll see some cracking or peeling where the resists are. Use an abrasive such as steel wool or sandpaper to rub the paint back and reveal those areas.

4. If you'd like, repeat the process, this time applying your resists to bare areas of wood as well as on top of the first coat of paint. Again, aim for 20–30% resist coverage, and brush on a coat of your second color.

5. Repeat the steel wool/sandpaper rub down, and make sure to brush all the dust away.

6. Give your piece a final coat of antiquing wax. It will mellow out the paint(s), stain any bare wood, and protect the finish. Wipe back any excess wax as you go, and buff it when dry.

TIP
Don't panic if too much paint comes off with a resist layer—now's the time to practice your dry-brush technique and "touch in" paint to the areas that might look too bare! If there is a heavy residue of the resist agent left on the surface, you may need to use the appropriate solvent to remove the excess.

1

6b

2

5

3

6a

The finished piece

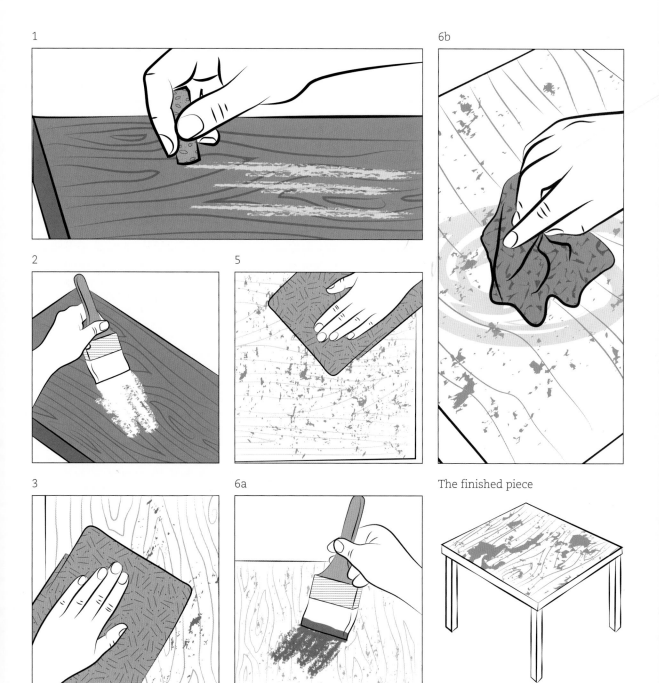

Tutorial
Whitewashing with milk paint

Decades ago, whitewashing was an inexpensive way to brighten up and protect exterior surfaces, but it had to be redone each year. Now, with milk paint, we can get that pretty, faded look easily indoors or out, and it lasts for ages!

Milk paint (or casein paint, as it's sometimes called) comes in a powder form. Mix it with water when you're ready to paint. Once mixed, it doesn't have a very long shelf life, so make just what you need as you go. The paint can be mixed 1:1 for an opaque coating, or up to one part paint and three parts water to be used as a wash, the way we'll do here.

A simple piece of furniture—primitive, even—in bare wood is ideal for this technique. If your furniture has been stained, that's fine too, but any varnish or polyurethane will need to be stripped off to let the wash soak in to the grain of the wood. You won't use primer for this method.

YOU WILL NEED

- Jar or small bucket
- Measuring cups or spoons
- Milk paint powder in white or off-white
- Warm water
- Whisk or stirrer
- Coarse bristled brush
- Rags
- 220-grit sandpaper
- Wax, tung oil, or hempseed oil

1. In a jar, mix the milk paint powder with warm water in a 1:3 ratio.

2. Use the whisk or stirrer to blend the paint thoroughly. Allow the mixture to sit for a few minutes so that all the pigment can dissolve, and then stir again.

3. Slather on a layer of the milk paint, one section at a time. The unsealed wood will absorb it.

4. Remove as much of the milk paint as you like with a rag while it's still wet, then move onto the next section.

5. After the paint has dried, rub the piece down gently with sandpaper to distress it and to even out the wash if necessary. Be sure to brush away any sanding dust.

6. Seal the piece with wax, hempseed oil, or tung oil. These old-fashioned top coats are appropriate for this style of finish—anything too shiny would take away from the look.

TIP
When mixing milk paint, you can use a whisk or stirrer to leave some small lumps in the paint, or put it through a blender to ensure a totally smooth consistency—it's really up to you and the look you're after: rustic and somewhat gritty, or more refined and smooth.

1

4

6

2

The finished effect

3

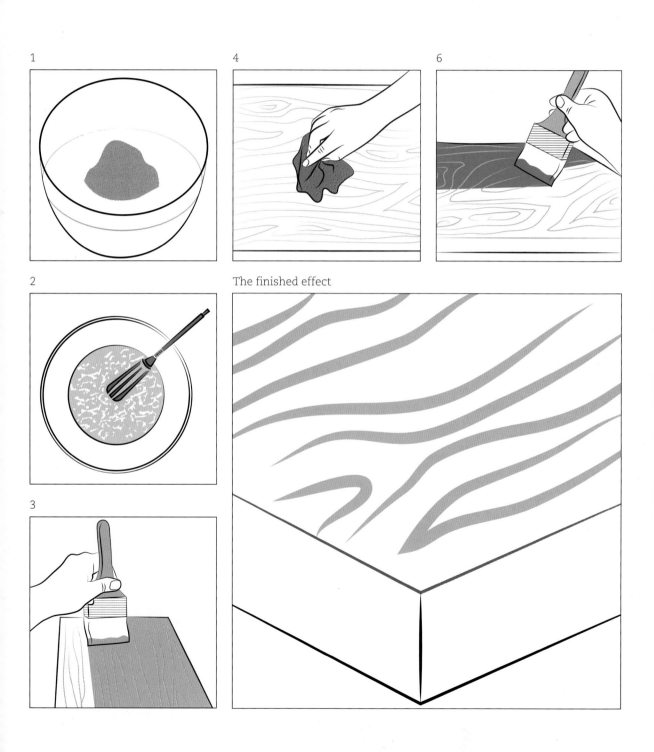

Case Study
Mignonne Décor

Painted furniture takes on a modern, edgy look in the talented hands of Johnelle Mancha, lead designer and owner of Mignonne Décor. With a clean silhouette and bold color choices, she created a true statement piece—one that will begin as a nursery changing table, but is sophisticated enough to work in a grown-up space later on.

Johnelle scooped this darling—but rock-solid—1950s piece at an estate sale for only $40. She recommends searching for one that has the right shape and scale for your space. On her frequent treks through flea markets, thrift stores, and estate sales, Johnelle is always on the lookout for clean-lined pieces with "good bones" that are well made.

She believes in highlighting the vintage aesthetic of a piece, but knows that sometimes her clients want to add bolder elements to a room—that don't read aged, worn, or rustic—to keep the mix interesting and a reflection of the individual.

She sanded down the piece to the original wood to give herself a clean slate. (Johnelle's tip: invest in a good sander!) Then, using a lighter color of flat paint, she primed the piece.

Next came several coats of her "pop" color (in this case salmon pink). Once those layers were dry, she used a ruler and pencil to trace a straight line for the division between the color and metallic paints, and then taped along the mark. She followed this with one more layer of salmon paint, covering the tape this time, too. This part of the process requires patience, but pays off when the clean, crisp edge is revealed!

Two coats of gold paint in the taped-off section went on next, and were given time to dry. She slowly removed the tape, pulling it off at an angle to prevent taking the paints with it, and then she sealed the whole dresser with a clear top coat for greater protection.

We painted over the entire piece and right over the tape with our main 'pop' color. Painting over the tape assures that any paint leaking through or under will be covered.

PAINT/COATINGS USED:
- Water-based flat paint as a primer/base coat
- A pretty, salmon paint in an eco-friendly formula from Benjamin Moore
- Ralph Lauren Regent Metallics in Gold
- An interior furniture-grade clear coat

OTHER TOOLS & SUPPLIES:
- Fine sandpaper
- A ruler
- Pencil
- Low-tack painter's tape
- Synthetic bristle brushes

TIME TAKEN:
Start to finish, including drying time between layers: 2 days

FOR TUTORIALS:
Priming, page 46
Creating patterns with tape, page 110
Metallic paints, page 58

All photographs by Johnelle Mancha.

Case Study
IAmNotARobot

Photographer, Chris Gatcum, uses his downtime to reinvent pieces of furniture and create one-off, three-dimensional art works under the pseudonym IAmNotARobot. A self-confessed magpie, Chris has a workshop crammed full of found objects just waiting to be reconfigured into new and unique creations. Rarely throwing anything away, Chris is the perfect example of upstyler and recycler.

> *Instead of MDF try reclaimed planks or pallet wood for a more rustic feel, or a sheet of high-gloss colored acrylic (Perspex) for maximum shine against a matte-finished frame.*

Chris pulled his daughter's outgrown baby cot out of their loft after a year of storage. Realizing that it was too good to toss, he cleverly reinvented it for her: a young lady obsessed with writing, drawing, and "going to the office." Combining the bed parts with a few thrift-shop finds that were on hand and some basic supplies from the hardware store, the result is one happy budding executive with her very own workstation.

The cot had been taken apart before its attic exile, making it easy to sand the pieces down and coat them with a stain-blocking primer to ensure that previous paint and some stubborn fingerprints wouldn't affect the finish. With his little executive pulling up her favorite chair, Chris put the main pieces together for a "fitting" to determine the proper height for the desktop. 18 inches (45 cm) was just right.

Since the bed was designed with a rail at each end that supports the platform, Chris had to simply unscrew the rails, raise them up to a level height, and then re-fasten the screws. He then used the MDF cut to size to cover the slats, and glued it into place. He also took care not to glue the rails so the desktop can be raised later on as his daughter gets older and grows taller.

Chris repurposed some wire shelves and a knife drawer, spraying them with flat black paint and affixing them to the desk as drawers and storage. Once assembly was complete, he painted the desk with two coats of a "fetching shade of bubblegum pink"—his client's request. Realizing that was just too much of a good pink thing, they decided to use black chalkboard paint to coat the desk top and one end insert, so that his daughter can not only draw at her desk, but on it as well.

PAINT/COATINGS USED:
- Stain-blocking primer
- Water-based matte-finish paint
- Spray paint (for accessory parts)
- Chalkboard paint
- Top coat of choice

OTHER TOOLS & SUPPLIES:
- 120-grit sandpaper
- Sheet of ¼ in (6 mm) thick MDF or plywood
- Tape measure
- Wood glue
- Screws
- Screwdriver
- Jigsaw
- Drill
- Wire shelves & drawer (thrift-shop finds)

TIME TAKEN:
Half a day to build plus a week, working on and off, for the painting

FOR TUTORIALS:
Repairing, page 48
Chalkboard paint, page 64
Fixes for hardware, page 92

All photographs by
Chris Gatcum.

Paint Techniques
Gallery

Top left: Chest of drawers by Margaret Shepherd Apple of me & mrs. jones/ photograph by Stephanie Jones; **Above:** Ombré chest of drawers by Stephanie Jones/photograph by Stephanie Jones; **Left:** Metal leaf accented dining chairs by Rachel Pereira of Shades of Blue Interiors; **Opposite:** Twist leg table distressed using resist layer by Jessica Bertel Mayhall of me & mrs. jones/ photograph by Stephanie Jones.

CHAPTER 5

Finishing Techniques

Overview

You've chosen, planned, cleaned, repaired, prepared, and painted—now you're ready for some final touches! The finishes you'll choose from in the following pages have different characteristics but a common basic purpose, which is to protect your painted surface. Remember: no painted finish is ever bulletproof. But care for your painted pieces with respect and a gentle touch, and they will last a long time.

Waxing is one of the best techniques for creating a durable, touchable finish. Buffing the wax when it's dry is key for bringing up shine and helping to harden the wax. A stained and varnished finish on a table, dresser, or buffet is gorgeous and classic, and the right way to restore valuable old furniture. Stain and top coat can also be used in a more modern way, combined with painted portions of a piece.

When adding patina, glaze will give the most subtle effects, but it needs a top coat. Pigmented waxes give you a two-for-one—antiquing and toning as well as sealing for protection. Stains are a great method for adding patina when you've done heavy distressing, because the stain will mellow out the paint and also give rich color to any exposed wood.

Add polish and shimmer to surfaces with gilding waxes—from lamp bases to old candlesticks to hardware, it's a super-easy way to glam things up. And, speaking of hardware, read on for some quick fixes for everything from knobs to hinges. Use those same techniques to transform the frames on pictures and mirrors, and on curtain rods and finials.

These are the techniques that will protect and pull your painted finishes together, and set your projects apart from the rest.

Opposite: Dresser given patina with antiquing wax by Jessica Bertel Mayhall of me & mrs. jones/ photograph by Stephanie Jones.

Tutorial
Waxing

Wax seals porous surfaces, protects them, and gives a lovely old-fashioned feel and gleam. Wax has the advantage of being easily repaired and touched up, but does need a little care. Depending on the use and cleaning a piece gets, you may need to reapply wax every few months or every few years.

All waxes contain solvents to make them workable, but some brands are more odor-free than others. Once the solvents evaporate, they leave behind a natural, durable coating. Make sure to have adequate ventilation while you're applying the wax, and allow several days afterwards for the wax to "cure" before the furniture gets heavy use.

Some materials will absorb more wax than others—flat or milk paints and unsealed, stained wood will drink up more wax than an acrylic/latex or alkyd paint. A second coat of wax may be applied for extra protection. Allow an overnight dry in between coats. Use a pigmented or tinted wax to give a soft or aged effect.

YOU WILL NEED
- A firm-bristled brush or a cloth for applying
- Clear paste wax or finishing wax
- Clean, lint-free rags for wiping and buffing

1. Load your brush or cloth with a teaspoon or so of wax. If it's too firm, let the wax sit in a sunny window or a pan of hot water for just a bit, as wax needs a comfortable ambient temperature to behave properly.

2. Apply a thin, even coat of wax to the surface, working one section at a time. If you see that there is excess wax sitting anywhere, wipe it away with a clean rag.

3. When the wax has dried (check the label for dry times—usually an hour to overnight), buff it to a shine with a lint-free cloth. Old sheets, cloth diapers, and oxford-cloth shirts work especially well as buffing cloths—you need something with a little heft to create the friction that hardens the wax and brings up the gleam. The more you buff, the shinier and more durable the finish will be.

4. Dispose of buffing rags properly after you've laid them out flat to dry—they will contain traces of the solvent from the wax, which can be combustible if left bunched up.

5. Take care of your waxed pieces by dusting gently, using a napkin under a wet glass or mug, and cleaning when needed with a mild soap and microfiber cloth. Aerosol sprays and harsh cleaners will lift and damage the waxed surface.

TIP
Wax must be at a comfortable ambient temperature to behave its best—cold will make it too firm, and excessive heat will liquefy it. Work indoors (with adequate ventilation) for the easiest process and best results.

1

2

3

5

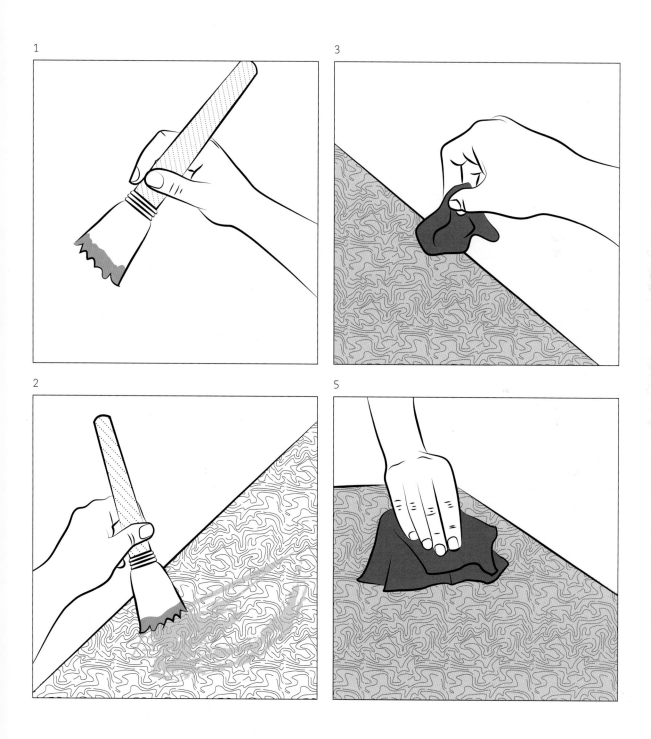

Tutorial
Staining and varnishing

Staining and varnishing wood surfaces—traditional refinishing—is the perfect treatment for pieces with attractive grain, inlays, or where paint or other coatings might compromise the value of the piece. It's especially practical for tabletops or other kinds of furniture that might see too much wear and tear to be a good candidate for paint. For staining, you'll need to begin with bare wood, so strip any existing paints or top coats (see pages 42–43 for instructions on stripping). A good sanding following stripping is essential.

Get creative: combine stained surfaces with paint (such as detailing stained wood with hand-painted or stenciled embellishments before varnishing), or keep the body of a dresser stained while adding color to the drawers with paint. Block out a pattern with tape (see pages 110–111) or a stencil (see pages 104–107), and use contrasting colors of wood stain.

Stains and top coats come in oil-based and water-based formulas. Choose the one that suits your project best—oil-based products are a little more durable over the long run, and are generally available in a wider variety of colors than water-based. Water-based stains can also raise the grain of wood, which will need to be smoothed down with sandpaper. Use oil-based polyurethane over water- or oil-based stain, and water-based top coats only over water-based stain.

Some woods require a conditioner or sealer prior to staining for an even finish, so follow the manufacturer's recommendations. Stir stain and varnish well before using. Avoid shaking, since it causes air bubbles that will affect your finish.

YOU WILL NEED
- Synthetic bristle brushes
- Stain
- Lint-free rags
- Varnish
- 120- and 220-grit sandpaper
- Vacuum
- Tack cloth or damp cloth

1. Working one section at a time and with the grain, brush on (or wipe on with a rag) a nice, even coat of stain, and allow it to soak into the wood for a minute or two.

2. Using a lint-free rag, wipe back the excess. If you'd like a darker finish, apply a second coat once the first one has dried. Allow the stain enough time to dry thoroughly.

3. Apply varnish or polyurethane, brushing it on in long, smooth strokes that overlap slightly. Don't put it on too heavily—two or three thin coats is best.

4. Sand gently with 220-grit sandpaper in between coats of varnish, removing the dust with a vacuum and then a tack cloth or damp rag.

TIP
Take care to keep your work space dust-free when varnishing. Allow an hour after sanding between coats for all the dust to settle so that you can wipe it away and keep your finish pristine.

1

2

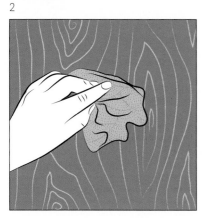

3

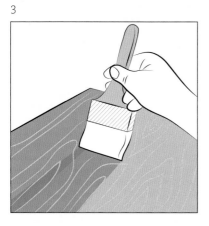

4

The finished piece

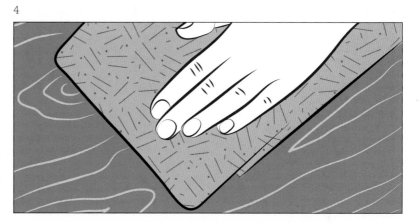

Tutorial
Adding age and patina

Why is it that it's important for us to look young, and yet we value a little age on our furniture? On some pieces, there is definitely dignity in having been around a little bit.

Several methods add the patina of age to painted furniture. Authenticity is key—avoid contrivance! A mellow, aged feel can be given with glaze, wax, or stain. The technique is basically the same for all three: brush or wipe on, and then carefully remove excess. Use oil-based glaze on either water-based or oil-based paints. Latex or acrylic glazing media will only adhere to water-based paint.

YOU WILL NEED - FOR DISTRESSING

- Rocks or a piece of brick
- Bolts, screws, nails, and/or keys
- A hammer
- Sandpaper in grits from 120–400
- Coarse steel wool

YOU WILL NEED - FOR GLAZING

- Glazing medium tinted with raw umber, or a pre-made "antiquing" glaze
- Natural bristle brushes—one kept dry
- A dense foam roller (optional)
- Cheesecloth
- A top coat such as varnish or polyurethane, or clear wax

DISTRESSING

Distressing adds another dimension. It's simply when paint is roughed up with tools and abrasives. Strive for authenticity. Study old painted pieces and note where wear typically shows: the edges of dresser tops and drawers, the bottoms of chair and table legs, and areas around hardware and pulls.

1. Use the rocks and tools to create wear and tear, focusing on the edges and lower areas, where dings and scuffs would occur over time. Tap in clusters of shallow nail holes to give the look of worm-eaten wood.

2. Use sandpaper or steel wool to ease the paint back at the edges, again taking care to create an authentic look. Sand primitive styles a little more vigorously, but give just a little gentle wear to more elegant looks.

GLAZING

A glaze is the most translucent choice and offers greater flexibility. Because you can tint it yourself (or have it tinted at the paint counter in the hardware shop) it's easy to control the level of pigment that is added. Glazes can be any color: a gray/white for a limed, bleached look; olive green for mossy effects on stone colors; or raw umber for a cool gray, aged appearance. Since glaze stays "open" or workable for a few minutes, it's easier to manipulate for more subtle looks.

Besides brushing, you can roll glaze on with a dense foam roller, and then pull the excess off with a rag or cheesecloth. Once you have a rag or cloth that's a little saturated with glaze, hold on to it—at the end of the glaze application, it's nice to add little spots of patina here and there by gently patting the surface with that cloth bunched up in your hand. Use a dry chip brush and feathery brushstrokes to "soften" areas that might have gotten too much glaze.

TIPS

Next time you're browsing old furniture, whether in shops or online, note where old paint takes the most wear and tear, and keep that in mind when distressing and aging your pieces: around the edges, the handles or pulls, chair backs, and the bottoms of legs and feet. Authenticity trumps perfection!

For an additional layer of age, use a "fly-speck" technique. Load an old toothbrush with your antiquing medium (glaze, stain, or thinned-down wax) and run a craft stick or your thumbnail across the bristles to spatter the surface here and there with patches of "specks."

Opposite: Aged cabinet, GAP Interiors/Emma Lewis.

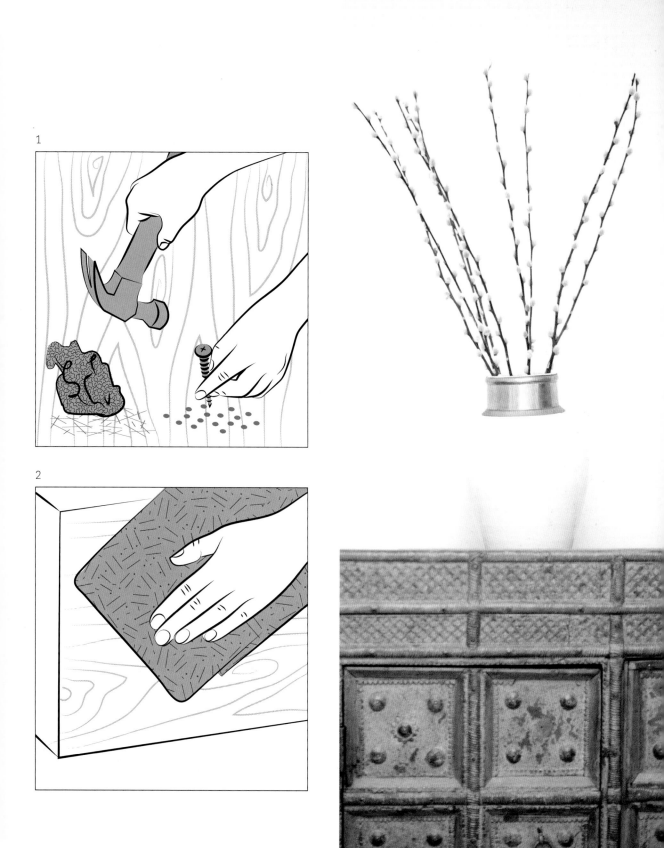

1

2

Tutorial
Adding age and patina continued

Pigmented waxes have the advantage of sealing your surface as well as adding color or patina. Colors within most brands can be mixed to tweak the tones. Woodworkers' supply shops and antique stores usually stock a variety. White-tinted "liming" waxes, as well as antiquing waxes in deep brown or raw umber colors, are great to have on hand.

1

YOU WILL NEED - FOR WAXING

- Pigmented wax in brown, black, or an "antique" tone
- A firm-bristled brush
- Shop towels or lint-free rags

YOU WILL NEED - FOR STAINING

- Wood stain in a mellow color, such as walnut
- Lint-free rags
- A brush

WAXING

Wax is a little heavier and less workable than glaze. Brush it on with a firm-bristled brush and a firm hand, and wipe it back and move it around as you go. It may take just a few passes to get your rhythm, but keep in mind that some clear wax on a fine steel wool pad or some mineral spirits will lift any excess or mistakes right off.

STAINING

Using stain as an aging glaze of sorts works really well on pieces that have had a lot of distressing done to them, since the stain will not only mellow the paint and give it a pretty patina, but it will also soak into the bare wood that's been revealed, staining it to a rich color.

As with other stained surfaces, a varnish or other protective top coat is recommended.

For glazing, waxing, and staining, the process is basically the same:

1. Working one section of your piece at a time, brush on an imperfectly even layer of glaze, wax, or stain.

2. Working quickly, wipe and pat the surface to remove the excess and to give the antiquing medium a faded, mottled look. Use a cheesecloth and a dry brush to soften the glaze, a sturdy rag to wipe back wax, and a lint-free cloth to move the stain around.

3. Leave a little more patina at the edges of your furniture, and on the bottoms of table legs and chair feet.

4. Apply a top coat to the glazed or stained pieces as desired. Buff waxed furniture to a soft gleam with rags.

2

Opposite: Distressed reclaimed apothecary chest. GAP Interiors/ Johnny Bouchier.

Tutorial
Metallic accents

Beyond metal leaf and metallic paints is another method for adding a bit of shimmer to furniture and hardware: gilding wax. A soft, spreadable, sparkly finishing touch, gilding wax comes in small tubes or pots in a wide variety of metallic hues, and packs a lot of punch for just a little bit of effort.

Trace a pretty detail, change the finish on knobs or pulls, or highlight a stenciled pattern by applying the wax with your finger or a small brush. Blend gilding wax with a clear soft wax to create a translucent shine over a large area. Use a tin or pewter wax over deep gray paint for a zinc-like look, or copper wax on top of a turquoise-verdigris color for a knockout patinated appearance.

Due to their somewhat delicate nature until they're totally dry and cured, gilding waxes need to be your very last touch on a piece. Applying other waxes or oil-based top coats over them will lift the shine right off. The silver lining is knowing that you can use a little dab of clear wax to tweak the gilding wax.

Brushes and other utensils will need to be cleaned with mineral spirits.

YOU WILL NEED
- Gilding wax in one or two shades
- Clear soft wax
- Plastic saucer and spoon or palette knife
- A 2 in or 3 in (5 cm or 7.5 cm) chip-style brush
- A small brush or cotton swab
- Soft rags

1. Mix a dab of gilding wax with a good dollop of clear wax, about one part to eight. Blend it well on the saucer, using the spoon or palette knife.

2. After the paint (and top coat, if any) has dried thoroughly, use the chip brush to sweep the wax on in a nice, even layer. Wipe back any excess with a soft cloth.

3. Allow the wax mixture to dry completely, and then buff to a shine.

4. On pulls, details, or a patterned area, use a small brush or cotton swab to apply full-strength gilding wax. Use a dab of clear wax on a cloth to fix any places that are too heavy.

5. Allow the wax to dry, and give it a good polishing with a soft cloth to bring up the shine and to help harden the wax.

TIP
Don't be afraid to blend colors to get just the metallic tone that you want. A bit of a bright gold leaf color mixed with silver will yield a lovely champagne-hued wax. Tone a platinum color down with black to get a mellow pewter. Experiment!

1

4

5

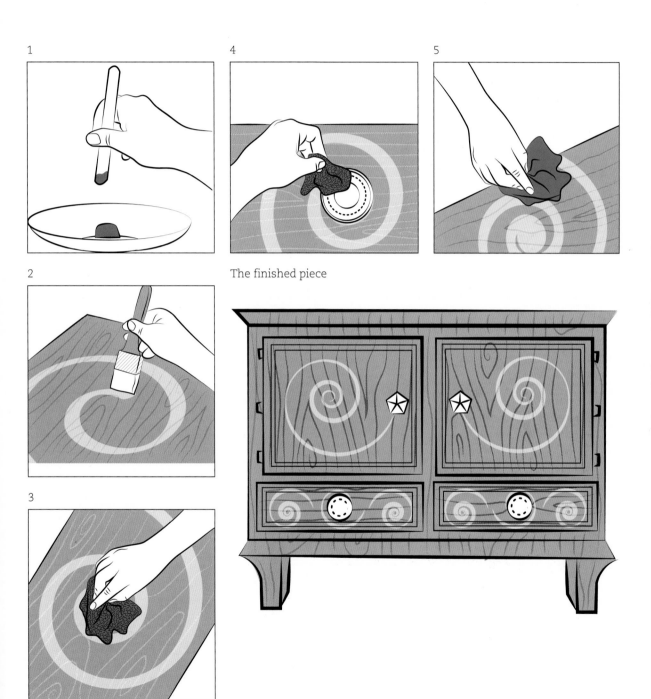

The finished piece

2

3

Tutorial
Fixes for hardware

The right hardware on a piece of furniture is much more than utilitarian. It's the detail that can elevate a piece from plain-Jane to knockout. When possible, it's good to reuse original hardware, maybe with a tweak or two. You'll be amazed at what fine steel wool, brass polish, and polishing with a soft cloth will do for neglected, crusted-over pulls!

If parts are missing or broken, salvage the good ones for another project and choose something new for your current project. There are endless choices for replacements made of ceramic, bone, and glass.

Besides good looks, hardware must function. Make sure that knobs, pulls, hinges, and other parts are sturdy enough for the job and installed correctly. Just a little wood filler and slightly longer wood screws can steady a rickety door. If the hole for a knob has become too big over time, a washer will help hold the nut in place. If you're stumped, snap a photo on your phone and find a helpful fellow at the hardware store. In a pinch, even strong jute twine can make a good-looking handle on a rustic piece.

When refinishing pulls, knobs, and the like, replace the screws in each piece, flip a sturdy box upside down, cut Xs with an artist's utility knife every few inches, and push the screws through the Xs. That way, they will sit up straight for painting or gilding and can be easily moved around for, say, spray-priming outside and finishing inside. Finials for curtain rods can be set up in the same way.

On ornate metal handles that need a fresh look, try a coat of high-bonding water-based paint. When the paint has dried to the touch, use an old washcloth dampened with water and gently rub the paint back on the raised details, revealing a little bit of the metal beneath.

Flip back to the tutorials on metal leaf, metallic paints, and gilding wax for specific instructions on changing a look from one metal to another. Peek around the spray paint section at the craft store for more easy fixes. Some paints may need a coat of primer made especially for metal applied first for the best adhesion—drawer pulls on an oft-used piece will see some wear, so make sure to use the correct undercoat. Metal primers come in spray form, which makes them super convenient.

Wooden knobs can be done up in a contrasting color, hand-embellished, gilded, painted to match for a monochromatic look, or stenciled. Use your imagination and unleash your creativity.

Opposite: Detail of a painted and distressed writing desk trimmed in gold leaf with gilt wax on the pulls by Elizabeth Humphreys Moore of me & mrs. jones/ photograph by Stephanie Jones.

Tutorial
Fixes for hardware continued

YOU WILL NEED

- Wooden knobs
- 220-grit sandpaper
- Cloths
- A sturdy box
- An artist's utility knife
- Primer
- Small paintbrush
- Paint
- Small stenciling brush
- Small-scale stencil
- Paper towel
- Top coat of your choice

1. Gently sand the knobs to knock any shine down. Wipe with a damp cloth to remove sanding dust.

2. Make Xs in the bottom of the box with the artist's utility knife, and push the knobs (with the screws still attached) through to hold them steady for painting.

3. Brush on a coat of primer, and when it's dry, apply two coats of paint, allowing drying time in between coats.

4. Load the stenciling brush with a tiny bit of paint, offloading the excess onto a folded paper towel.

5. Holding the stencil on the top of the knob, pounce the paint through the stencil openings.

6. Sand gently, if desired, to soften the pattern. Top with wax, poly, or varnish to protect the finish.

1

2

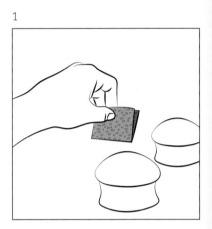

3

TIP

When hunting for a replacement pull or knob, check with a local junk dealer or antiques restorer to see if they have a stash of cast-offs and odd pieces you can look through—you may get lucky and find exactly what you are looking for!

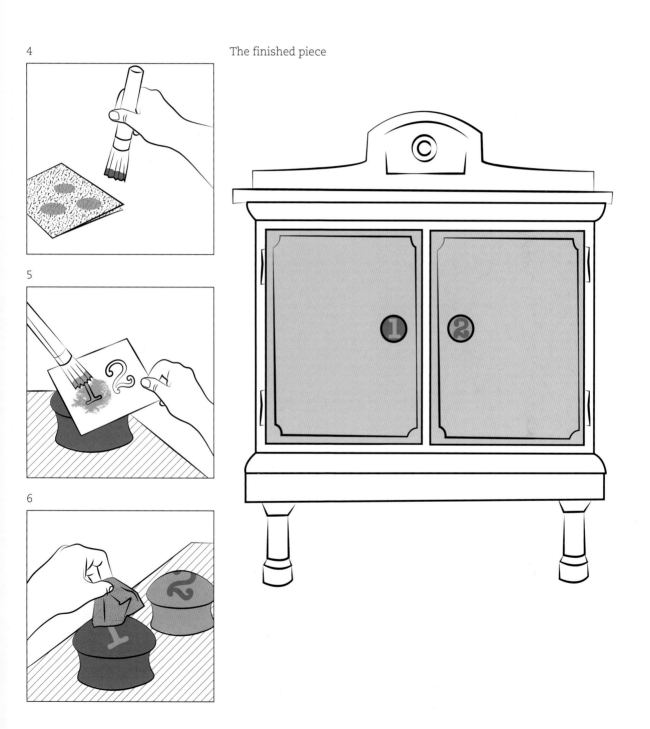

4

5

6

The finished piece

Case Study
My Kind of Refined

University student Meriweather Adams is already an accomplished DIYer, having challenged herself to decorate her dorm room (and now apartment) with a lot more creativity than cash. She writes about her decorating and adventures in DIY on her beautiful blog, My Kind of Refined.

Layered paint and a rustic farmhouse look are favorites of hers, and a multi-colored distressed milk-paint finish is the perfect way to achieve that look. Meriweather scored this chair at a local thrift shop, though you may have a similar piece in your attic already.

She mixed the milk paints in empty containers, using a spoon and measuring the paint powder in to warm water at a ratio of about 1-to-1. The first coat was Ironstone, a sheer white, that she used almost as a wash. The next color, Eulalie's Sky, was a good, consistent coat, mixed a little more thickly with a bit more powder and a little less water. Once that coat was dry, Meriweather smoothed the paint lightly with fine sandpaper so that any variations in the pigments blended together a bit.

Next on, a coat of Luckett's Green, a color named in honor of the renowned Old Luckett's Store in Virginia, USA. She sanded lightly again, this time distressing down to the other paint layers in places, and revealing a tiny peek of bare wood in others. After removing all the sanding dust, she slathered on a generous coat of hemp oil using a chip brush, wiping back

> *Steel wool is one of the best distressing tools—not only does the milk paint look softly 'worn,' but it gets burnished to a soft sheen, too.*

PAINT/COATINGS USED:
- Miss Mustard Seed's Milk Paint in Ironstone, Eulalie's Sky, and Luckett's Green
- Hemp oil

OTHER TOOLS & SUPPLIES:
- Chip brushes
- A hair dryer
- Fine sandpaper (220-grit)
- Medium-grade steel wool
- A hand-mixer or whisk
- Small measuring cup
- Empty container or jar
- T-shirt rags

TIME TAKEN:
An afternoon

FOR TUTORIALS:
Distressing, page 70
Whitewashing with milk paint, page 72

All photographs by Meriweather Adams.

with a T-shirt rag. Over the oil went another layer of green, which peeled and chipped a little due to the resistance of the oil—again, in a very attractive way! To enhance chipping, either let your piece dry in warm sunlight, or apply heat with a hair dryer.

Meriweather finished the chair by giving it a rub-down with steel wool, focusing on areas that would naturally receive wear and tear over time to make her distressing authentic, concentrating on the seat, the front stretcher, and the fronts and backs of the chair legs.

Case Study
Les Couronnes Sauvages

The intrepid, endlessly creative Claire Chalkley is the proprietress of Les Couronnes Sauvages, located in Dol-de-Bretagne, France. Primarily a floral designer, Claire also delights in the transformation of furniture with her favorite medium Chalk Paint®. She scored this pair of robust but unremarkable and generic office chairs for a song. Their saving grace: the backs and seats come off with the undoing of a few screws.

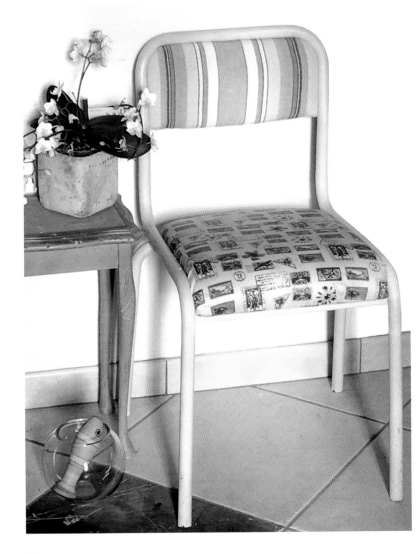

With a swipe of ammonia-based cleaner to remove any dust or grime, she "crashed past the boring preparation phase" and jumped right into the painting. The first coat was dry enough after a cup of tea that she could apply the second coat. Claire advises "traveling" with the brush, not just resting it in one place—lay the paint on and keep moving along.

Once the paint was dry, she used a brush to work in some clear wax, just a little at a time, smoothing it over like a body cream without too much pressure. After wiping the excess wax off with a lint-free cloth, she left the wax to dry and pulled out her staple gun.

Using oilcloth and the seats as a template, Claire traced the shape of the seat onto the back of the fabric, leaving a good, wide margin all the way around. She cut the cloth and centered it on the seat, turned the edges around to the back, and stapled it on.

She then made a little pocket to slip over the back, again by tracing the shape of the seat back onto the wrong side of the fabric. This time, Claire left a 2-in (5 cm) margin on the top and

> *By turning a chair upside down to begin painting it gives you a fighting chance of not missing any annoying parts while painting. So turn it over. And paint it.*

sides, and a 4-in (10 cm) one on the bottom. Using her sewing machine, she stitched up the sides and top, turned it right-side out, slipped it over the back plate, and then hand-stitched the bottom edge, with the edges of the fabric tucked neatly inside and therefore hidden.

After reattaching the seats and backs, Claire advises that now is the "ta-dah moment": sit back and enjoy.

PAINT/COATINGS USED:
- Chalk Paint® decorative paint by Annie Sloan, in Old Ochre and French Linen
- Clear Soft Wax by Annie Sloan

OTHER TOOLS & SUPPLIES:
- Screwdriver
- Firm-bristled brushes for painting and waxing
- Lint-free cloths
- Fabrics from Papa Pique Maman Coud and Annie Sloan
- Scissors
- Staple gun and staples
- Sewing machine
- Needle and thread

TIME TAKEN:
About a day to paint, wax, and re-cover two chairs

FOR TUTORIALS:
Waxing, page 82
Easy embroidery techniques (for hand-stitching), page 130

All photographs by Claire Chalkley.

TIP
When stapling, begin with one staple at the center of each side, making sure the fabric is sitting straight and not pulling one way or the other. Then, work your way around, tucking the corners under neatly as you go.

Finishing Techniques
Gallery

Left: Green chest with patina by Jessica Bertel Mayhall of me & mrs. jones/photograph by Stephanie Jones; **Above:** Stained and varnished swan chair by Stephanie Jones/photograph by Stephanie Jones; **Below:** Buffet with metallic accents by Julia Miller of 551 East Design; **Opposite:** Table with painted accents by Catherine Denton Wilfong of me & mrs. jones/photograph by Stephanie Jones.

CHAPTER 6

Stenciling, Printing, and Texturing Techniques

Overview

Now that you've gotten this far with your project, it's time to add another layer to your finish. Some factors to consider: Are there other patterns or textures in the room? Fabrics or a rug that need something with a little "wow" in order to hold their own in the mix? How is the piece constructed? Are there flat surfaces that would be easy to apply pattern to, that will act as your canvas? Raised trim, lots of carving, panes of glass, and curvy spots can be difficult to work around. Is the furniture clean-lined, modern, and masculine? Or is it curvy, delicate, and feminine? Choose a treatment that suits the style of the piece.

In planning a color scheme for the pattern, think about the mix in the rest of your space, and choose something that will stay in balance with the other elements. Too bright or deep a color could give a piece more visual weight than it can carry.

Ever since people have been cobbling together furniture, they have been devising ways to dress it up with stains and paints, even using pigments suspended in a substance like yogurt and rubbed into the wood. Inexpensive, less-refined lumber has been finished to resemble more expensive and rare woods, as well as marble, tortoiseshell, and stone. In other words, embellishing furniture to elevate a space is nothing new—there are just faster and easier ways of getting it done these days! Look to history—from folk art to art deco—as inspiration for all sorts of transformations with applied pattern.

Opposite: Stenciled and color-blocked table,
GAP Interiors/Colin Poole.

Tutorial
Making stencils

Creating a consistent pattern is so much easier when you have a template to follow. While there are tons of terrific stencils to buy ready-made, it's easier than you might think to cut your own when your motif is simple.

Search online resources for graphics and ideas, and have a friend with good image editing software help resize an image to use. A block letter, geometric shape, or silhouette is a nice starter project. Once you've printed out the design, you're ready to begin.

Make sure that your sheet of mylar is at least 2 in (5 cm) larger all around than the design you'll be using. You need a good margin! A thicker piece of mylar will be sturdier if you're doing lots of repeats of the pattern, but thinner mylar will be much easier to cut and handle.

YOU WILL NEED

- Pattern printed on paper
- A sheet of clear mylar, 3 to 5 mm thick
- A permanent marker
- A cutting mat (or pieces of cardboard larger than your design)
- An artist's utility knife and/or small, sharp scissors

1. Find, resize, and print an image to use for your stencil.

2. Place the mylar on top of the paper with the design in the center. Use the marker to trace the outline onto the mylar leaving at least 2 in (5 cm) border around the image.

3a. With the mylar on the cutting mat, use the artist's utility knife to carefully cut along the traced line.

3b. Depending on the pattern, it may be easier to begin in the center with an X-shaped cut, and then use small scissors to cut the design.

TIP
Cut a second stencil with a detail to lay over the first pattern, such as adding a flourish to a fleur-de-lis, or a monogram over a silhouette, in a contrasting color.

1

2

3a

3b

Tutorial
Painting with stencils

Adding pattern to a piece with a stencil can take your painted furniture to a whole new level of style. Employ a plain, boxy dresser as your canvas and express yourself: cute and sweet, tailored and sharp, or elegant and sophisticated. Florals, damasks, houndstooth patterns, typography—let your creativity run free.

Repositionable spray adhesive will help keep a stencil from sliding around, but it won't seal it tight enough to keep an overloaded brush from pushing paint under the stencil, blurring the pattern. To prevent seepage, take care to use just a little bit of paint at the tips of the bristles, and swirl the brush around on a folded paper towel to off-load excess paint before beginning to pounce the paint into the pattern. Using a "dry brush" like this means that the paint will dry very quickly, so for a more solid pattern, it's easy to build up another layer or two of paint. Just don't try to fill it in with one brush load.

The best stenciling brushes have flat "heads" and soft, thick bristles. Choose a size that suits the scale of the pattern you're using—one too small will waste effort and muscle, and one that's too big can make a mess by going out of bounds and putting paint where it doesn't belong.

Once you've found a stencil and base-coated your piece of furniture, it's time to take the plunge.

YOU WILL NEED
- A stencil
- Low-tack spray adhesive
- Low-tack painter's tape
- Acrylic paint
- A stenciling brush
- A paper towel folded into quarters
- Cotton swabs
- 400-grit sandpaper (optional)

1. Spritz the back of the stencil with low-tack adhesive and allow it to dry for a few minutes.

2. Position the stencil where you'd like the edges to be, and secure it with tape if necessary.

3. Load a tiny bit of paint on the brush and then off-load any excess on the paper towel. The brush will be just barely wet.

4. Stipple the paint into the stencil openings with a pouncing motion. If you'd like the pattern to be more opaque, add a second layer of paint as soon as the first one is dry.

5. Clean up any blurry lines or seepage with a damp cotton swab or the corner of a paper towel.

6. To fade the pattern back, sand very gently with fine sandpaper.

TIP
For a pattern that has a repeat, you'll need to use whatever "registration marks" the stencil designer has given you. On some, small motifs from the pattern will appear as "windows" at the edges of the mylar, allowing you to match the pattern. Others may have a cutout shape at each corner of the sheet that you'll fill in with a pencil, and then match up as you continue the pattern.

1

4

The finished piece

2

5

3

6

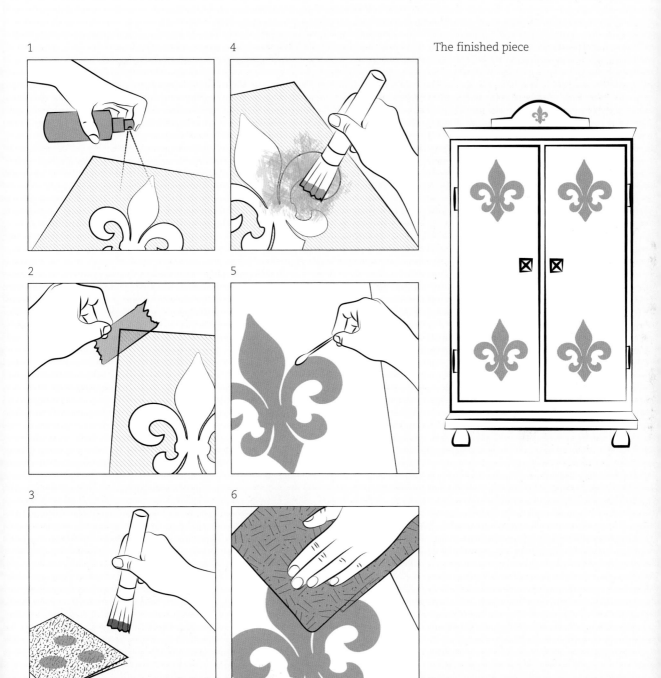

Tutorial
Spray painting on glass

Painting and gilding on the reverse side of glass is an age-old technique known as *verre élgomisé*. A quick, modern version can be achieved using spray paint and tape, contact paper, or a stencil to create a pattern.

Changed your mind about the look or color scheme? Not a problem, as the paint can be removed with solvent so you can put a fresh idea to work.

YOU WILL NEED

- Flattened boxes or drop cloth
- A piece of glass cut to size
- Painter's tape, contact paper, or a stencil for creating your pattern
- Spray paint in at least two colors (since glass can have a greenish cast, choose hues that won't be affected by a tinge of green, or warmer colors to counteract the cool tone)
- Cotton swab
- Mineral spirits
- Rubber bumpers or felt pads

1. Protect your work area with flattened boxes or a drop cloth. The over-spray from spray paint can get quite messy—it's a great project to do outdoors on a calm-weather day. If you must work inside, make sure you have adequate ventilation. Use a piece of glass cut to fit your tabletop.

2. Decide on the pattern you'd like to create. Here, we used wide painter's tape to block out a chevron design.

3. Spray the taped side of the glass in even, sweeping strokes, holding the can the distance directed on the label. Work from side to side or up and down, whichever is most comfortable—just keep the spray can moving smoothly to avoid blotches and drips. Release the spray cap at the end of each stroke.

4. Carefully remove the tape as soon as the paint is dry to the touch. Use some mineral spirits on a cotton swab to touch up any spots in the pattern where paint may have seeped under the tape.

5. Using your second color, spray paint again to fill in the areas that had been taped or covered. The paints will overlap on the working side, but when flipped over, the pattern will be nice and crisp.

6. Once the paint is completely dry (overnight is best—it may feel dry to the touch, but allow plenty of time for the paint to dry thoroughly), apply felt pads or rubber feet to the painted side, flip upside down, and put the glass in place.

TIP

Make sure to follow the manufacturer's instructions on the spray paint label as to re-coat and dry times—often, you'll need to either work the next layer in quickly or allow an overnight dry. Due to the high solvent content, adding more paint in between times can cause bubbling or blotches. Spray paint needs to either be freshly applied or fully dry to accept another coat.

1

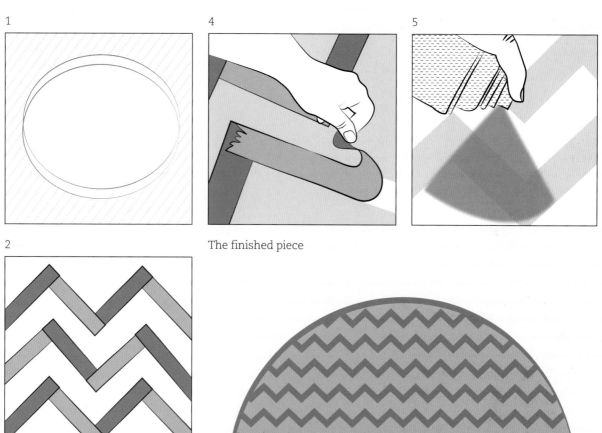

4

5

2

3

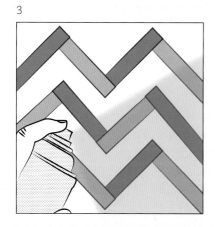

The finished piece

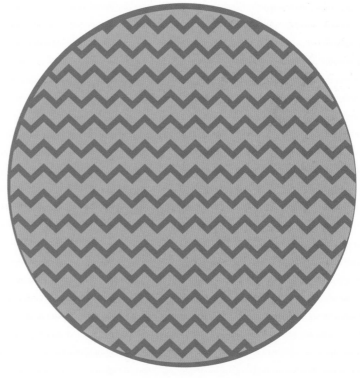

Tutorial
Creating patterns with tape

With the new shaped tapes and delicate-surface painter's tapes on the market, creating a crisp pattern with paint has become a cinch.

Browse the Web or hardware stores for precut tapes in chevrons, scallops, and other patterns, and use your imagination and the lines of the piece you're embellishing as inspiration for other linear designs. Awning-style stripes, Mondrian-inspired color blocks, a randomly patterned stained-glass effect, and even classic looks like a Greek key are all easy.

For a little more randomness, tear the tape lengthwise to create texture and a more organic look. Zebra or tiger stripes can be done with torn strips of tape, as well as a sort of "waves-upon-the-shore" effect. Make sure to burnish the edges of the tape to prevent seepage. To do this, push down firmly to remove any air bubbles and to ensure good adhesion. If you're painting lots of pattern, putting your thumb inside the bowl of a plastic spoon and running it down the edges of the tape lets you push a little harder for a tighter bond. Remove tape before the paint is completely dry, otherwise some water-based paints will pull away and remain attached to the tape instead of the surface. "Delicate surface" tape should not remove your base coats of paint when you reveal your pattern.

YOU WILL NEED

- A ruler and/or T-square
- Pencil
- Sharp, small scissors
- Delicate-surface (low-tack) painter's tape
- A plastic spoon
- A contrasting paint color for your piece
- Small artists' brush or narrow sash brush

1. Measure 5 in (12.5 cm) in from each corner of a square or rectangular surface, and mark with a pencil. Measure 1 in (2.5 cm) in along the edges, and mark occasionally along the length.

2. Carefully lay down strips of painter's tape along the 1 in (2.5 cm) marks, stopping at the 5 in (12.5 cm) marks. At those corners, run the tape in toward the center of the surface until the pieces meet, forming a nice, neat, squared-off corner.

3. Lay a second pattern the same way, leaving 1 in (2.5 cm) open inside the first taped lines.

4. Burnish the edges of the tape with your thumb in a plastic spoon, pushing down to make a good bond for crisp lines.

5. Double-check the angles with the T-square to make sure they are perfect.

6. Carefully brush on paint inside the tape. To prevent any seepage, two light coats of paint with ample dry time in between is better than one heavy coat. Pull off the tape before the paint has dried completely.

TIP
It's worth the trip to the hardware store to pick up some "delicate surface" painter's tape for this technique—don't use that old, sticky roll of masking tape you just found at the back of the garage cabinet! The residue it can leave behind (or the paint it may pull off with it) isn't worth the trouble you'll save.

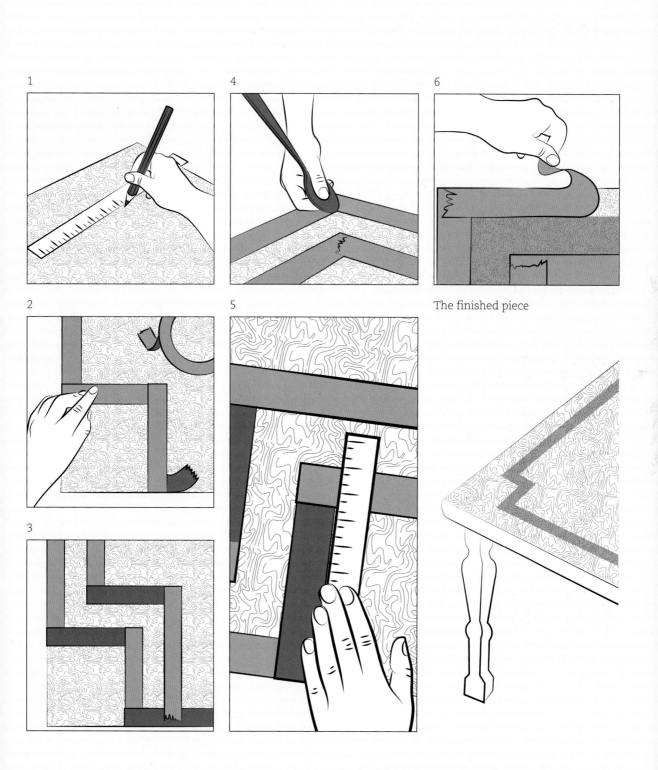

1

2

3

4

5

6

The finished piece

Tutorial
Designing your own decals

Hooray for technology! With the explosion of available fonts, typography software, ink-jet printers, and specialty papers, making your own decals has become easy to do at home.

Experiment with layouts and designs until you come up with something you like in the size you want, and then hit "print." Try a monogram, geometric pattern, or something fun and typographical—just keep in mind that simpler lines are best, since you'll be cutting these out by hand. More detail will require more patience!

Visit an office supply or craft store to pick up the right water-slide decal paper for your home printer and you'll be ready to go.

1

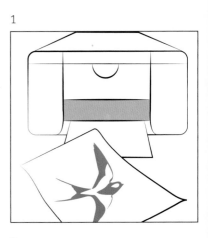

YOU WILL NEED

- Water slide decal paper
- Spray fixative (follow the recommendation of the paper manufacturer)
- Scissors
- An artist's utility knife
- A cutting mat (or plywood or cardboard)
- A shallow bowl of warm water
- A scraping and smoothing tool such as a spatula
- A soft, lint-free cloth or T-shirt rag
- Clear polycrylic water-based top coat (optional)

1. Finalize your desired design, and print it out onto the water decal paper's glossy side. Remember to set your printer to "photo paper."

2. Spray the decal with the fixative and allow it to dry, following the directions on the label.

3. Carefully cut out the decal, using either the scissors or the utility knife on a cutting mat or piece of plywood.

4. Immerse the decal in the bowl of water—it should curl up. When it is laying flat again, you're ready to go.

5. Carefully slide each decal off its paper backing.

6. Lay it into place on your piece. Working very gently with the spatula, from the center of the decal, squeeze out any air bubbles and excess water.

7. Pat softly with the cloth to dry the area. Allow to dry thoroughly. Protect with a layer or two of polycrylic, if desired.

2

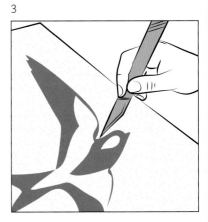

3

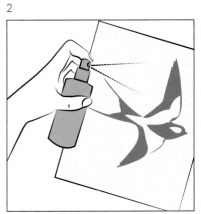

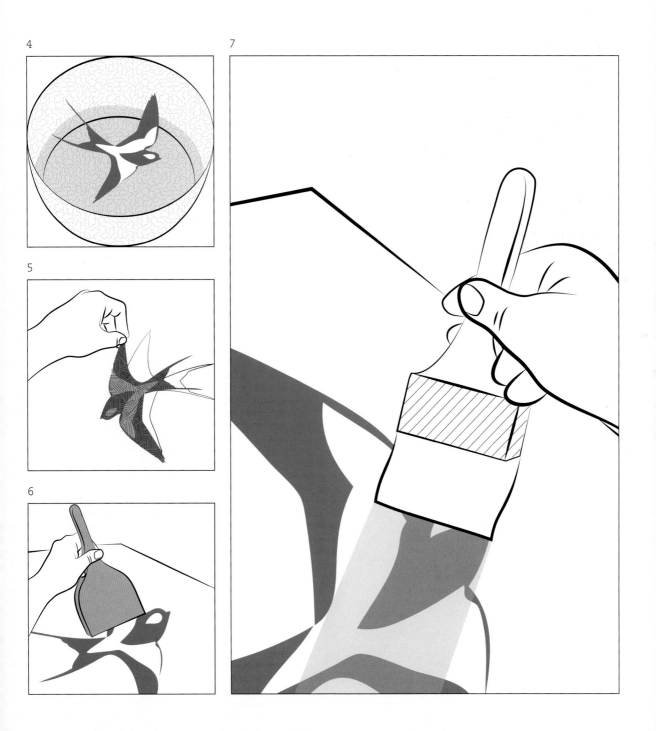

Tutorial
Block printing

Block printing is a relief-printing technique for adding pattern to a surface area. Historically, the blocks have been made from wood and other soft, easily carved materials. Block printing has been used on everything from silks in ancient China to printing books to contemporary artwork.

Printer's linoleum is a fantastic material for creating blocks to print with, and is readily available at art supply and craft stores. It is easily carved with some basic tools, and can be glued onto a wooden block for sturdiness on bigger projects with more repeats.

Simple, geometric motifs are good to start with and very effective when repeated. Keep in mind that your pattern will print in the reverse of the way the block is cut, and that only the uncut portion of the block will take the paint to the surface. Linoleum cuts more easily when it's warm, so a gentle going-over with a hair dryer on low heat can help the carving go more smoothly.

If a stop at the grocery store is easier than the craft shop, grab a potato or carrot. You can cut the potato in half and then apply the same steps shown here. Remember though, vegetables absorb ink and paint differently than cork so practice on some rough surfaces first.

YOU WILL NEED

- A "block" of either linoleum, a vegetable, or a cork
- A fine-tip permanent marker
- Carving tools such as a craft knife or artist's utility knife, or a linocut carving set
- Water-based paint
- A shallow, flat container or plate
- Cotton swabs

1. If you're using a vegetable as your printing block, cut it to create the size you need for your print, and allow it to drain and dry a bit on paper towels.

2. Decide on a pattern to use as your motif, and trace it or draw it onto the block with the marker.

3. Cut into the block around the outline of your pattern. Carefully (always cutting away from you) cut away the material around the motif, leaving only what will create the print.

4. Spread a little bit of paint into a shallow saucer or pan that has a flat bottom. Dip your printing block straight into the paint to load the raised area as evenly as possible, being mindful not to overload.

5. With nice, even pressure, apply the block to the surface to transfer the paint.

6. Reload the block with paint, and repeat to create your pattern. Clean up any smudges or mistakes with a damp cotton swab.

TIP

Hunt around at flea markets and vintage shops for patterns to use in your projects. It's not unusual to find carved wood printing block fragments from Asia, old typesetting pieces, or elaborately patterned rollers used for wallpaper or to emboss clay for gilding—any of which would make terrific ready-made printing materials.

2

3

4

5

6

Tutorial
Decoupage

Decoupage means "to cut," and is a technique that you can use to great creative advantage on furniture. Book pages, maps, wrapping paper, wallpaper, magazine pages, scrapbooking papers, and letters—even thin fabrics—make terrific materials to cut and apply to drawer fronts, chair seats, tabletops, and more. You can always scan and copy images to use if the originals are valuable.

Your images can stand on their own, be scattered around a surface, or overlapped for a wonderful layered patchwork. You can use a decoupaged surface as a base layer for other treatments like stenciling and gilding, too.

Air bubbles can form beneath the paper, but don't panic—they usually subside when the decoupage gel or glue has dried. A brayer, the small firm roller used in printmaking, is a great help in pushing the paper down flat on the surface, though a craft stick, popsicle stick, or bone folder also work in a pinch.

YOU WILL NEED
- Paper or fabric to cut and use
- Sharp scissors
- A pencil
- Matte decoupage medium, made for paper
- Small brushes for spreading the glue
- A printmaker's brayer or a craft stick
- A top coat of your choice

1. Cut out the images or pages you're going to glue to the surface. Lay them out in place to firm up your design. If needed, make soft pencil marks as guidelines for placement or alternatively take a quick photo of it to refer to.

2. Spread a thin, even layer of decoupage gel or medium onto the area to be covered with your choice paper or fabric.

3. After allowing the gel or glue to set for just a few minutes, place the cutouts where they belong, pressing down gently.

4. Working from the center out to the edges, smooth the cutouts into place, working out any air bubbles with a brayer or a craft stick, and making sure the edges are not lifting up.

5. Continue layering and gluing the cut-out pieces until your design is complete. If you're adding any other layers, such as stencils or metal leaf, make sure everything is thoroughly dry, otherwise the damp paper may tear.

6. Once the glue underneath the cutouts has dried, brush another thin layer on top of the paper or fabric. When it's fully dry, apply a top coat to your whole piece with a varnish, wax, or polyurethane.

TIP
You may need to employ a straight pin from your sewing box to burst any larger, stubborn air bubbles—then, gently smooth the paper into place as you push the air out using the brayer.

1

2

4

5

6

3

The finished piece

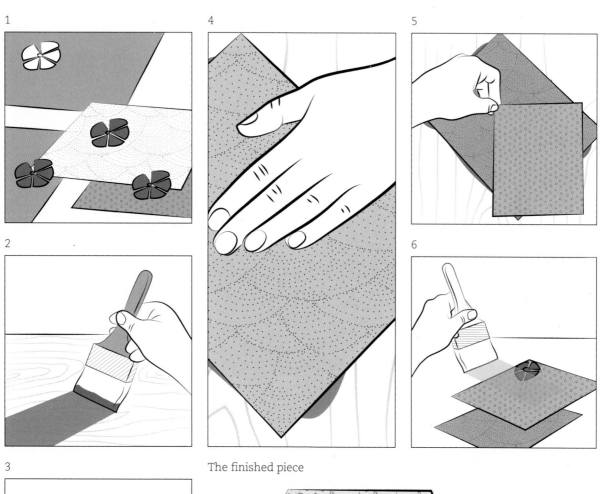

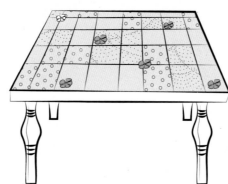

Tutorial
Adding hand-painted details

Don't let the thought of hand painting some lovely details onto your furniture intimidate you! You've got this. This tutorial includes some little "cheats" to help ensure success. However, soon you'll be working without the net. While using a stencil or tape gives your patterns nice, crisp outlines and edges, don't underestimate the power of a charming, perfectly imperfect embellishment.

Just the ticket for bringing attention to a simple, boxy piece, or for calling attention away from not-so-fabulous features, hand-detailing comes toward the end of the painting part of a project, but before any distressing, aging, or sealing.

The craft store has plenty of decent-quality artists' brushes to use, as well as small containers of acrylic paint perfect for adding touches onto furniture done in water-based paint. Over oil-based paint, an oil-based medium should be used.

Let folk art, chinoiserie, tribal patterns, bone inlays, and nature be your inspiration. Here, we're going to create a simple boxed pattern with French corners to get you started.

YOU WILL NEED

- Low-tack painter's tape, 1 in (2.5 cm) in width
- A short ruler or tape measure
- A pencil
- A small bowl or mug
- A small, firm-bristled artists' brush
- Small pot of paint in a color that coordinates with your piece
- 400-grit sandpaper

1. Using the edge of your piece as a guide, lay a strip of painter's tape down around each side of a tabletop or drawer front, or other rectangular or square section of furniture 1 in (2.5 cm).

2. With a ruler and pencil, make a mark 4 in (10 cm) in from each end.

3. Place the mug or bowl upside down so that the edge touches the pencil marks at each corner, forming a rounded shape at the corner.

4. Lightly trace around the bowl with a pencil, making an elegant "French corner" detail.

5. Load an artists' brush with paint, and using the tape as a guide (not as a template), paint alongside—but not touching—the tape.

6. When you get to the corners, follow along your penciled line. Reload the brush as necessary. The lines will be sort of uneven and wonky, and the paint will be heavier in some areas than in others—that is okay.

7. Remove tape. Gently ease back the painted lines with fine sandpaper, using it to "erase" any spots that are too heavily painted, and then apply a top coat as desired.

TIP
To ease your way into a more elaborate hand-painted design, use a pencil to trace lightly around the edges of a stencil pattern, and paint the design with a narrow artist's brush and contrasting paint color.

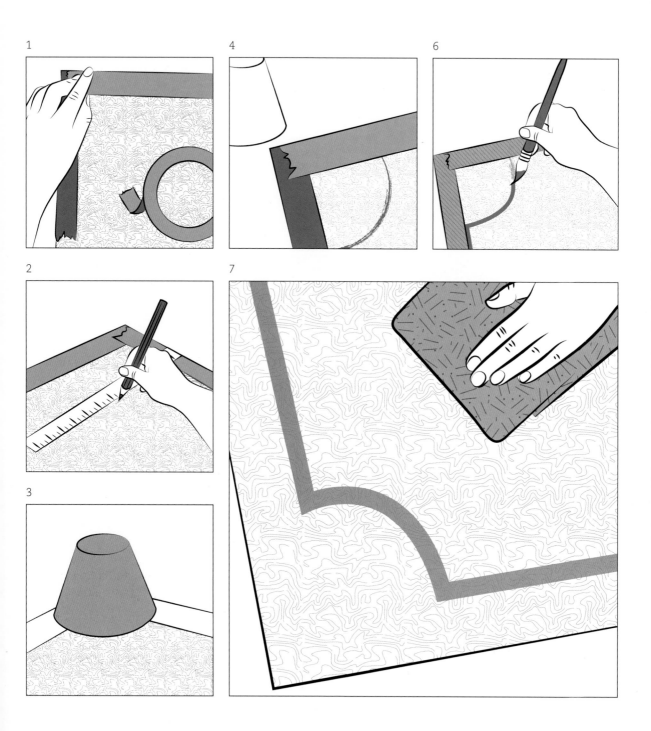

Case Study
Mols & Tati-Lois

Primarily a creator of gorgeous hand-tailored, "statement" lampshades as Mols & Tati-Lois, Natalia Price-Cabrera is also a visual daily diarist and freelance editor. In some of her rare spare time, she upstyles furniture using paints and fabrics, and gets very lucky with online auction site and thrift-store finds!

Natalia recognized the potential in this four-drawer chest, and snapped it up for $16 because of its beautiful lines. After cleaning it up and removing the few drawer pulls it had, Natalia used wood glue to repair a couple of the drawer runners, and then gave it a coat of primer.

Once the undercoat was dry, she applied the first coat of paint, using Vanille for the drawers and Winter Sky for the body. Employing loose, free brushstrokes perfect for this type of paint, Natalia had the first coat on quickly. A quick rub down with 120-grit sandpaper prepared the piece for a second coat of paint. Once that was completely dry, it was time for Natalia's favorite part of the process—distressing—because "that's where the finish takes shape."

She always begins with a going-over of the whole piece, using fine sandpaper, to remove any excess paint. Then, because Natalia prefers a "bold, beaten-up look" she goes back more forcefully with medium-grit paper, in this case rubbing back quite a bit on the body of the chest of drawers.

Happy with the degree of distressing she'd created, she then cleaned the dust away and began waxing, applying

PAINT/COATINGS USED:

- An undercoat/primer
- Autentico chalk paint in Vanille and Winter Sky
- Clear wax
- Dark wax
- Top coat

OTHER TOOLS & SUPPLIES:

- Paint brushes
- Wood glue
- Kitchen sponge
- Coarse and medium-fine sandpaper (60–120 grit)
- Lining paper or wrapping paper
- Vintage drawer pulls
- Hammerite rust remover
- Wire wool
- Screws
- Spray mounting adhesive

TIME TAKEN:

A day and a half, including drying time

FOR TUTORIALS:

Waxing, page 82
Adding age and patina, page 86
Fixes for hardware, page 92

All photographs by Chris Gatcum.

> *Speed up drying time by using a hair dryer on the piece in between coats of paint.*

clear wax with a kitchen sponge cut in half. To add accents and depth to certain details on the piece, Natalia used a dark wax, focusing on the moldings at the bottom and on the front legs. She encourages fearless experimentation with the dark wax, since a little clear wax and a firm hand can help blend and take the dark wax down a notch, or remove it altogether. She let the piece dry overnight to begin the curing process for the wax, and then applied a matte top coat as a final layer.

As finishing touches, Natalia added "collected" hardware and lined the drawers. She'd hunted down several beautiful (but intentionally mismatched) drawer pulls, again scoring great deals on some tarnished, rusty pieces with pleasing shapes. She freshened those up using rust remover and steel wool, a lot of patience and a little love. Using spray mount adhesive, she lined the drawers with a vintage-style wrapping paper for a slightly sweet and "ditsy" feel.

With a little scouting, effort and time, and not a lot of expense, Natalia rescued a lovely old piece, giving it a little old-school charm and restoring its dignity.

Stenciling, Printing, and Texturing Techniques
Gallery

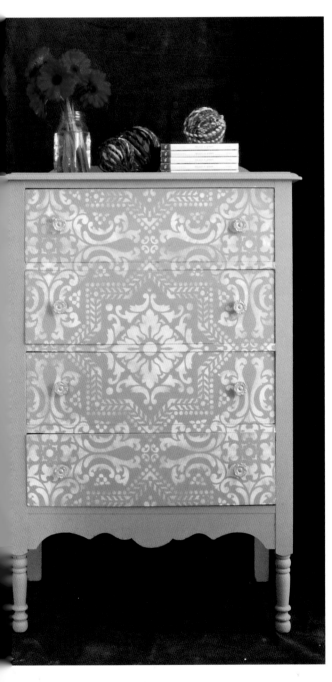

Left: Dresser with white stencil pattern by me & mrs. jones/photograph by Stephanie Jones; **Top:** Herringbone stenciled desk by Rachel Pereira of Shades of Blue Interiors; **Above:** Bird and branch hand-painted dresser by Rachel Pereira of Shades of Blue Interiors; **Opposite:** Chest of drawers stenciled with Roman numerals by Charlie Jones and Stephanie Jones of me & mrs. jones/photograph by Stephanie Jones.

CHAPTER 7
Embellishing Upholstery
Overview

Sometimes that perfect project piece has one little problem left to solve—parts of it are upholstered, or need to be. Just as you've found with painting and finishing, a simple, custom fix can be very simple to achieve!

In some cases, the existing fabric might need just a little jazzing up, which is where applying trims such as braid, pom-poms, or tassels will save the day. Whether you heat up the glue gun or thread a needle, it's going to be easy. No tassels or pom-poms on hand? Not a problem—they are simple to make yourself.

Have a canvas drop cloth or length of burlap around? There is a blank canvas just waiting for something special! Try block-printing a pattern on, or create some bold, colorful embroidery. Or, use a contrasting scrap of something else to create an appliqué. You might even combine several of these techniques for a layered look.

If the fabrics on hand aren't large enough, piece them together using cross stitches or running stitches with a brightly colored embroidery thread or thin ribbon. And, if what's around needs perking up, don't be afraid to try dyeing material.

Cheerful, old-fashioned patterns such as Toile de Jouy or gingham are widely available and can lend a classic, sweet, or elegant touch to a piece. Check the closet as you could find an old sweater, flannel blanket, or chambray shirt that can be pressed into service. Well-worn flat-weave rugs such as kilims can also do double-duty as a heavyweight fabric. Keep in mind that a light or sheer fabric doesn't make a good candidate for upholstery, so skip past the "curtain" fabrics and shop the upholstery-weight section instead. Choose a material that suits the piece you're working on.

Opposite: Patchworked upholstered headboard and frame, GAP Interiors/Colin Poole.

Tutorial
Adding trims, pom-poms, and tassels

Collectively, trims such as tassels, pom-poms, and gimp have been known historically as *passementerie*. As fancy as the name might sound, these trims can be used to hide staples and glue, and in fresh and modern ways, too—so don't pass on the passementerie!

Trims will take that basic piece to a whole new level of pretty, and the application itself doesn't have to be major surgery. Most of the time, a few simple stitches, some iron-on bonding strips, or a bit of hot glue is all you need.

Consider creating feed-sack stripes or a Greek key pattern with bands of grosgrain ribbon, or using pom-poms along the edge of a lampshade, cushion, or curtains. Here, we're going to make some tassels and use them to liven up a chair seat.

YOU WILL NEED
- Your choice of fabric scraps, eyelash or other fancy yarn, ribbon, and/or twine
- Scissors
- A ruler
- An embroidery needle and thread

1. If using fabric, cut it into strips that are ¾ in (1.9 cm) wide and 8 in (20.3 cm) long. Cut ribbon, yarn, or twine into 8 in (20.3 cm) lengths also.

2. Each tassel will require 14 strips, ribbons, or pieces of yarn or twine. Group together a pleasing arrangement of colors and textures.

3. Lay the strips out with all the ends even. Using another piece of ribbon or twine, tie the bundle in the center with a double-knot.

4. Fold the bundle in half, and tie another of your extra strips around the whole bundle about ¾ in (1.9 cm) down from the top. Secure it with a square knot (tying the right strand over the left, and then the left over the right).

5. Work the ends of the tie to mix in with the rest of the tassel. Trim the ends even if necessary.

6. Thread the needle, knotting the end, and use a few stitches to tack and secure the tassel into place. Once finished, secure to your chosen piece of furniture.

TIP
You might also string the tassels along a longer piece of twine or yarn to use as a garland, or secure them to either end of a strip or strand to tie around a doorknob, to tie back curtains, or to decorate a chair back.

1

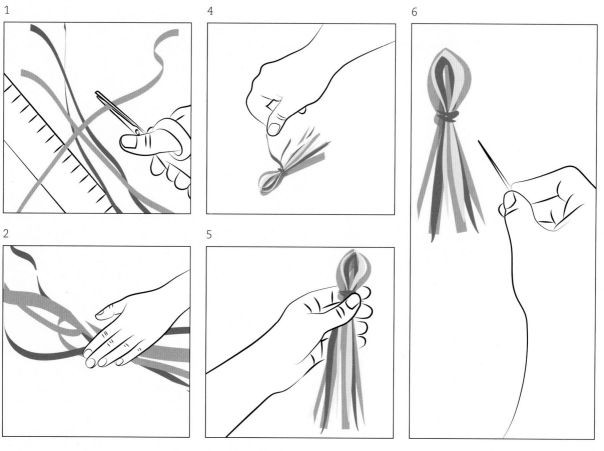

2

3

4

5

6

The finished piece

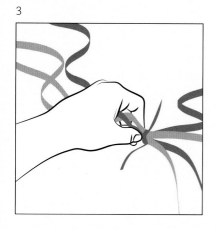

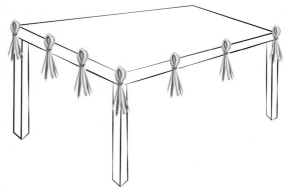

Tutorial
Fabric printing

Block printing onto fabric is very similar to printing onto a painted surface, as in the tutorial on pages 114–115. Antique printing blocks carved into wood in a range of fabulous patterns can be found at flea markets and vintage stores.

If you'd rather create your own pattern, that's easy to do, too. Carve a linoleum block or potato, or use a ready-made object such as a cork (for polka-dots) or the top of a Styrofoam cup (for circles). The spine of an old book might even be used to make a herringbone or chevron pattern. Look around your kitchen as there are all kinds of things just waiting to be dipped in paint and stamped onto fabric!

Having a wide, smooth work surface is a big plus on a project like this, especially if you can spritz it with low-tack adhesive to help hold the fabric in place while you work. The side panel of a large box laid on the floor, or a big table protected with butcher's paper or Kraft paper would be perfect. The repositionable adhesive leaves a little residue behind, so cover your work surface carefully.

Just as in dyeing, natural-fiber fabrics such as cotton and linen that have been prewashed will take the paint much more thoroughly and evenly.

Refer to the instructions on page 114 for carving a block of your own.

YOU WILL NEED

- Flattened cardboard boxes or paper
- Repositionable, low-tack spray adhesive
- Fabric for your project
- A block or object for printing
- Water-based paint
- A shallow, flat container or plate
- Paper towels

1. Spritz your work area (protected with paper or cardboard) with low-tack spray.

2. Smooth the fabric into place on the surface.

3. Pour a little bit of paint onto the plate, and spread it around. Dip your printing block carefully into the paint so that only the raised area of the motif is coated. Keep in mind that any paint being carried on the block may end up on the fabric, so take care to touch only the area to be printed to.

4. Offload any excess paint onto a folded paper towel, and then firmly and evenly press the block onto the fabric, transferring the paint. Reload the block and continue printing until your pattern is complete. Then allow the paint to dry thoroughly. Your fabric is ready to use!

> **TIP**
> To see if your fabric requires pre-washing before printing, throw a few drops of water on it. If the water beads up, it would be best to wash, so that the "sizing" (a finish added by the manufacturer) can be removed for better results with paint. If the water soaks in, you're good to go. By the way, adding fabric softener to the laundry process when you're planning to paint is a no-go—a softener will prevent even absorption.

1

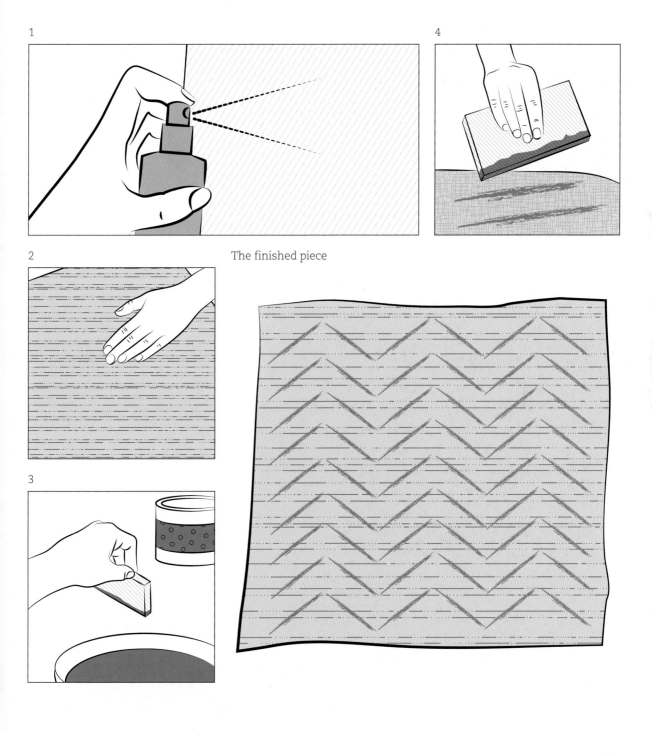

4

2

The finished piece

3

Tutorial
Easy embroidery techniques

Just a little handwork can elevate simple fabrics to something really personal and special. With a bit of practice, you will be able to master several basic stitches that will add a custom-made touch to your pieces.

Running stitch is an even line of stitches that weave in and out of the cloth. It's most often used to join two or more thicknesses of fabric together, but can be decorative as well. (You'll use a running stitch to embellish an appliqué on pages 132–133.)

Satin stitch is when long running stitches are snuggled up very close together, creating the effect of a solid spot of color. Take care to pull the thread through at an even tension, so that the stitched areas don't pucker.

Cross-stitch is just as it sounds—making Xs with a needle and thread. It can be functional as well as decorative, joining two pieces of fabric with a little flair, or creating a pattern on a single thickness. Run a row of stitches that slant one way, and then work back up the row, crossing all the Xs.

Ready to give embroidery a try? Let's go! We're going to create a sort of bohemian patchwork using pieces of fabrics that work well together.

YOU WILL NEED
- A few pieces of different fabric
- Fabric scissors
- An iron (optional)
- Straight pins
- An embroidery needle
- Thread in contrasting colors

1. Lay out your design on a flat work surface, making sure that the pieces overlap enough to be stitched together. You may need to rearrange the pieces several times until you find the mix you are happy with.

2. This step is optional: if the fabrics are very prone to fraying or you want a neater look, turn the edges under ¼ in to ½ in (0.6 cm to 1.3 cm) and press with the iron.

3. Pin the pieces into place, using the straight pins. Thread the needle, knotting the end of the thread.

4. Now, have fun! Experiment with thread colors and alternate stitching methods to create a crazy-quilt look. Pull in leftover pieces of ribbon and trims to stitch on, too.

5. Add a little satin stitch detail in spots, if you'd like.

1

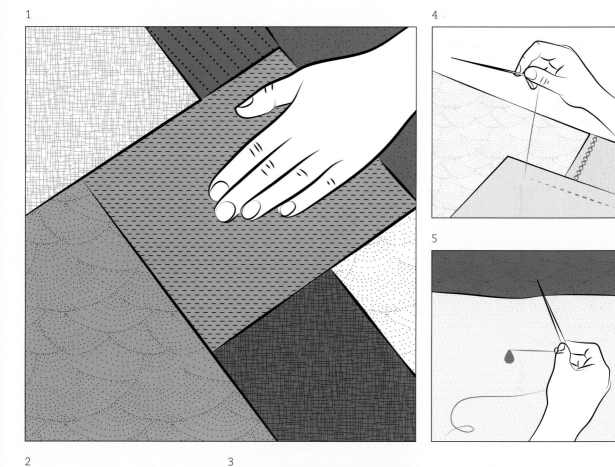

4

5

2

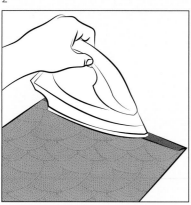

3

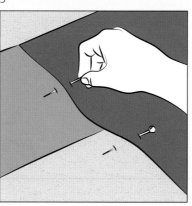

TIP
Make embroidery relaxing and enjoyable (and spare some sanity) by using the correct needles and embroidery floss or high-quality thread—ask for advice at the fabric or craft store so that you're taking home the right thing.

Tutorial
Appliqué

Stitching one layer of fabric to another is the basis for appliqué techniques. From simple to sophisticated, appliqué is a flexible way to stretch your creativity.

Follow a pattern that's in the fabric already, or create your own design. A monogram, a silhouette, or the outline of your favorite country or state are all fun ways to use this technique. Tuck the edges of the appliquéd piece under, and stitch perfectly and neatly, or leave raw edges showing and use loose, carefree stitches instead.

For this project, we were inspired by the generations-old Alabama-style handwork that's being revived by Natalie Chanin and her coterie of talented seamstresses in and around Florence. A project like this is easy and makes a great statement on a chair seat, seat back, or cushion cover.

1

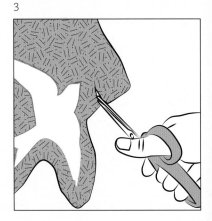

2

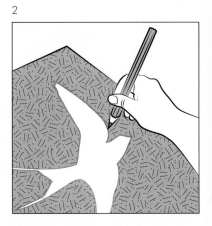

3

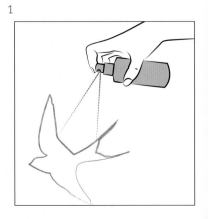

YOU WILL NEED

- A stencil in a simple design
- Low-tack adhesive spray
- Contrasting fabric for the pattern
- A chalk pencil
- Small, sharp embroidery scissors
- Base fabric large enough to cover the desired surface
- Straight pins
- Embroidery needle
- Thread in a matching or contrasting color

1. Spritz the back of the stencil with the low-tack spray and allow it to dry for a minute.

2. Place the stencil on the contrasting fabric and smooth it into place. Using the chalk pencil, trace the pattern around the edges of the stencil.

3. Cut the contrasting fabric around the pattern, leaving a little room around the chalk lines you've drawn.

4. Place the patterned piece onto the base fabric so that your pattern sits in the right spot. Secure it with a few straight pins.

5. Thread the needle, knot the end of the thread, and sew along the chalk lines, using a straight running stitch.

6. Once you've stitched up all the lines, knot the thread. With the embroidery scissors, trim the fabric around the pattern, about ¼ in (0.6 cm) from your stitches, leaving the raw edge to outline the design.

4

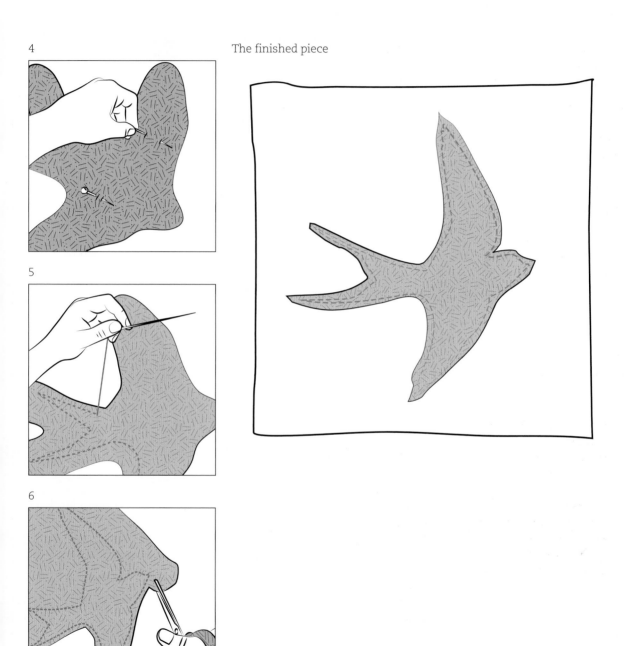

5

6

The finished piece

Tutorial
Fabric dyeing

Dyeing fabric is easier, more fun, and less messy than you might think! It's the perfect way to reuse old linens, such as tablecloths or large napkins, that you might happen to find at estate sales and junk shops. Dye also gives you the means to customize inexpensive materials like plain, light-colored canvas drop cloths and white burlap.

Natural-fiber fabrics such as cotton, linen, and silk take dye very well. Synthetics or blends that contain man-made materials will resist dye, so it's important to know your fabric's fiber content. Prewashing before dyeing is always smart as it helps get the fibers ready to accept the color and will give you a more saturated and even result.

There are many ready-to-use fabric dyes available widely at craft and hobby stores, fabric shops, and even the drugstore. It's also easy to find recipes for concocting your own dyes using fruits, vegetables, and spices from your garden or the grocery store. You can even use coffee and tea. Some paints can also be diluted and used as dye.

Over-dyeing is using a strong color bath to change a printed material into shades of one color. Old, faded fabrics are great candidates for over-dyeing projects—well-worn plaid flannel shirts and even flat-weave patterned rugs are popular "befores" for over-dyeing.

Ombré, dip-dyed, and wax-resist patterns are all other techniques to explore. Shibori is a traditional Japanese method for binding, stitching, folding, or twisting cloth to create patterns with dye, similar to what we call tie-dye.

Indigo, with other shades of blue and violet, were the most common hues seen in Shibori techniques, which have been used for hundreds of years. Let's give a basic Shibori technique a try with some fabric that we'll use to cover a chair seat.

YOU WILL NEED

- Drop cloths to protect your work area
- A piece of cotton or linen fabric, prewashed, and dried
- A pole: a length of bamboo or PVC or other plumbing pipe
- A strong rubber band
- Masking tape
- Cotton twine
- Two large tubs or containers
- Fabric dye, in liquid or powder form
- Measuring cup and spoons
- A large spoon, paddle, or stirrer
- Rubber gloves
- Washing machine
- Iron

1. Wrap the fabric around the pole.

2. Hold one end in place with a rubber band, and using masking tape, secure the other end to the pole.

3. Starting at the taped end, tie the twine tightly around the end and begin to wrap the twine around the fabric, scrunching the fabric down as you go. The tighter the twine, the more defined the pattern will be. When you get to the end of the roll, tie the twine off tightly.

4. Soak the wrapped pole in a sink or bucket full of warm water as this makes it easier for the fabric to accept the dye. While the fabric soaks, mix the dye according to the package directions.

5. Immerse the fabric in the dye bath and let it sit for a few minutes as instructed on the package. (This might be three minutes to an hour, depending on the dye.)

6. When time is up, rinse the fabric in cool water. At this point, the color will be much deeper than the final result. Unwrap the fabric, carefully unwinding it from the pole. Keep rinsing until the water runs clear. Machine wash the fabric in warm water with mild detergent. Dry it flat and press with a warm iron.

1

4

6

2

5

3

The finished piece

Case Study
11 Magnolia Lane

Christy Black is part of the inspiring team who blog as 11 Magnolia Lane. Her military family moves every year or two, which takes its toll on their furnishings. Christy has wisely decided to just go with the flow, using a painted and distressed finish to freshen up her dining room furniture. Her family loves the lighter, more casual feel of the room, now that it's not full of heavy, dark, damaged wood.

Before

After

Her staple gun was indispensable for this project, earning the rank of Very Best Friend, followed closely by her staple remover. Mindful of her budget, she took advantage of the yummy oatmeal color and inexpensive yardage of painters' drop cloths, and pressed them into service as upholstery fabric.

After cleaning, painting, distressing, and waxing the furniture, Christy got down to the business of recovering the chairs. She used the existing cushions as templates for cutting the canvas, and then slowly and carefully stapled the fresh fabric into place, taking care to keep the staples hidden. To finish them, she heated up her glue gun and

added gimp trim around the edges of the backs to hide any errant staples, giving the chairs a clean, finished look.

Being a monogram fan, Christy decided to add a rustic-looking "B" to the chair backs, using a fabric transfer technique. After creating the letter in

> *For the fabric transfer process, you'll need to find an older-model copier or printer that uses toner. I made my copies at the local public library!*

PAINT/COATINGS USED:

- Chalk Paint® decorative paint by Annie Sloan, in Pure White
- Soft Wax by Annie Sloan in Dark and Clear
- Citrasolv Natural Cleaner and Degreaser
- Scotchgard

OTHER TOOLS & SUPPLIES:

- Canvas drop cloths, pre-washed and ironed
- Monograms, flipped horizontally, and printed using toner
- Gimp trim
- Hot glue gun and glue sticks
- Scissors
- Staple gun and staples
- Staple remover
- Masking tape
- A small artist's paint brush
- A spoon

TIME TAKEN:

8 hours to paint and wax the table and chairs

8 hours to recover and monogram the chairs

FOR TUTORIALS:

Fabric printing, page 128
Distressing, page 70
Waxing, page 82

All photographs by Christy Black.

a font and scale that she liked, she "mirrored" it using photo-editing software, and printed out six copies on the copier at her library—an old machine that uses toner, a key to the technique.

Centering a "B" on each chair back, printed side down, she secured the top of the paper with masking tape,

flipped it up, and used the artist's brush to apply Citrasolv over the letter. She then flipped it back into place and rubbed the paper with a spoon vigorously to transfer the ink onto the fabric.

She applied a thorough coat of Scotchgard to protect the fabric, and the chairs were ready to go.

Case Study
Eats, Knits & Weaves

Kate Lancey-Smith is the "knits" half of the clever Eats, Knits & Weaves team, a British company specializing in treats for the home and palate. "Upknitting" furniture is her fresh twist on upcycling. She keeps a keen eye on dumpsters, thrift stores, and yard sales for finds such as this old telephone table, which she grabbed up because of the graceful curve at the back and for its "brilliant knit potential."

The first step in rehabbing an old piece like this of unknown provenance is a good cleaning. Kate uses natural products: vinegar, baking soda, and warm water. After bathing, a little repair was in order. Using small braces cut from scrap wood and carpenter's glue, she firmed up the wobbly joints. (Kate can't work a project without wood glue!)

Confirming her suspicion—using a magnet—that the door handle was indeed brass, Kate used her Grandma's tried-and-true method for cleaning it. In a small bowl, she combined the juice of half a lemon and a spoonful of baking soda into a paste. With a little patience—and more than one application—the brass was soon shining again.

Kate prefers the quick-to-dry finish of Chalk Paint® and loves that you can skip over the sanding and undercoating steps. Using bold and almost-clashing colors is a signature of her work. Plenty of masking tape around the cupboard door kept her edges nice and neat.

After the painting comes her favorite part of the transformation—the knit. Kate uses 100% British wool for her projects, here choosing a mix of

> *"To test to see if something is brass, use a magnet—even a fridge magnet will do. Solid brass is not magnetic."*

PAINT USED:
- Chalk Paint® in a bright, bold color combination
- Clear wax

OTHER TOOLS & SUPPLIES:
- Baking soda
- Vinegar
- Kitchen cloth
- Handsaw
- Spare wood scraps
- Wood glue
- Paint brushes
- Masking tape
- Sandpaper
- Kitchen sponge
- Soft dusting cloth
- Bicarbonate of soda
- Lemon juice
- Small bowl
- Graph paper
- Measuring tape
- Hard-wearing wool for knitting
- Knitting needles
- Sewing needle and thread
- Scissors

TIME TAKEN:
A week, working on and off

FOR TUTORIALS:
Distressing, page 70
Waxing, page 82
Easy embroidery techniques, page 130

Jamieson's Shetland wool and Texere chunky yarn—hard-wearing wools durable enough for a seat cover. She searched her knitting dictionary for the right stitch, creating swatches to try out the look. With the chosen swatch—one worked in "heel stitch," perfect for the wear a seat will get, and also for the beautiful texture—she used the sample to work out how many stitches she would need to cover the cushion. Graph paper came in handy for the next step: ensuring that the stripes would line up with the rods on the back.

With the knitting done and the paint dry, Kate was down to the finishing touches—sewing up the loose ends of the wool and attaching it to the old cushion using a needle and matching thread, and distressing and waxing the paint. Finally, using a kitchen sponge, Kate applied clear wax over her paintwork and buffed it to a matte sheen with a soft dusting cloth. Though the days of sitting still while conversing on a corded landline phone are gone, there is still plenty of room in the cell-phone driven home for a bold statement piece like this one!

All photographs by Chris Gatcum except top left on this page by Kate Lancey-Smith.

Embellishing Upholstery
Gallery

Left: Detail of cushion, GAP Interiors/Bill Kingston; **Top right:** Classic window seat, GAP Interiors/Tria Giovan; **Bottom:** Fabric detail chair, GAP Interiors/House and Leisure; **Opposite:** Upholstered bed, GAP Interiors/Costas Picadas.

SECTION THREE

Resources

Supplies

FOR PAINTS, PREPARATION SUPPLIES, TOP COATS, AND RELATED SUNDRIES:

Designer Paint
www.designerpaint.com

Dulux
www.dulux.com

Farrow & Ball
www.farrow-ball.com

Home Depot
www.homedepot.com

Lowe's
www.lowes.com

Sherwin-Williams
www.sherwin-williams.com

FOR MILK PAINT, CHALK PAINT®, TUNG OIL, HEMP OIL, AND WAXES:

Annie Sloan
www.anniesloan.com

Homestead House
www.homesteadhouse.ca

Miss Mustard Seed
www.missmustardseedsmilkpaint.com

Mylands
www.mylands.com

Real Milk Paint
www.realmilkpaint.com

FOR MYLAR, FINE BRUSHES, AND OTHER ARTISTS' SUPPLIES:

Blick Art Materials
www.dickblick.com

GreatArt
www.greatart.co.uk

Lawrence Art Supplies
www.lawrence.co.uk

Utrecht Art Supplies
www.utrechtart.com

FOR STENCILS, STENCILING BRUSHES, AND RELATED SUPPLIES:

Henny Donovan
www.hennydonovanmotif.co.uk

Maison de Stencils
www.maisondestencils.com

Royal Design Studio
www.royaldesignstudio.com

Stencil Library
www.stencil-library.com

Wallovers
www.wallovers.com

FOR GILDING SUPPLIES AND RELATED PRODUCTS:

Cass Art London
www.cassart.co.uk

Gold Leaf Company
www.goldleafcompany.com

Gold Leaf Supplies
www.goldleafsupplies.co.uk

Sepp Leaf
www.seppleaf.com

FOR METALLIC PAINTS:

Modern Masters
www.modernmasters.com

Plaid www.plaidonline.com

FOR WOODWORK SUPPLIES, REPAIR MATERIALS, TOOLS, STAIN, AND TOP COATS:

Rockler Woodworking
www.rockler.com

Rutlands
www.rutlands.co.uk

Woodcraft
www.woodcraft.com

FOR CRAFT MATERIALS:

Hobbycraft
www.hobbycraft.co.uk

Hobby Lobby
www.hobbylobby.com

Joann Fabric & Craft Stores
www.joann.com

M&J Trimming
www.mjtrim.com

Michael's
www.michaels.com

Purl Soho
www.purlsoho.com

The Craft Shop
www.the-craft-shop.co.uk

Previous page and opposite:
Photograph by Neal Grundy.

Further reading

The $50 Home Makeover
Shaunna West
Adams Media (July 2014)

Alabama Stitch Book
Natalie Chanin
Stewart, Tabori & Chang
(March 2008)

**American Decoration:
A Sense of Place**
Thomas Jayne
The Monacelli Press (October 2012)

**Bright Bazaar: Embracing Color for
Make-You-Smile Style**
Will Taylor
St Martin's Press (April 2014)

**Color Recipes for Painted
Furniture and More**
Annie Sloan
CICO Books (March 2013)

**Decorate: 1,000 Design Ideas for
Every Room in Your Home**
Holly Becker and Joanna Copestick
Chronicle (April 2011)

Design*Sponge at Home
Grace Bonney
Artisan (September 2011)

**The Design Cookbook: Recipes for a
Stylish Home**
Kelly Edwards
Medallion Press (May 2013)

Domino: The Book of Decorating
Deborah Needleman
Simon & Schuster (October 2008)

Farmhouse Modern
Terry John Woods
Stewart, Tabori & Chang
(October 2013)

Flea Market Fabulous
Lara Spencer
Stewart, Tabori & Chang
(September 2014)

**The Furniture Bible: Everything You
Need to Know to Identify, Restore &
Care for Furniture**
Christophe Pourny
Artisan (November 2014)

Furniture Makeovers
Barb Blair
Chronicle Books (April 2013)

Good Bones, Great Pieces
Suzanne McGrath & Lauren McGrath
Stewart, Tabori & Chang (May 2012)

I Brake for Yard Sales
Lara Spencer
Stewart, Tabori & Chang (April 2012)

Inspired You
Marian Parsons
Thomas Nelson (November 2012)

Modern Vintage Style
Emily Chalmers
Ryland, Peters & Small (April 2011)

Paint Magic
Jocasta Innes
Frances Lincoln (August 2006)

**Quick and Easy Paint
Transformations**
Annie Sloan
CICO Books (March 2010)

Remodelista
Julie Carlson
Artisan (November 2013)

**Spruce: A Step-by-Step Guide to
Upholstery and Design**
Amanda Brown
Storey Publishing (October 2013)

**Stencil It: 101 Ideas to Decorate
Your Home**
Helen Morris
St. Martin's Griffin (November 2011)

Style, Stitch, Staple
Hannah Stanton
Running Press (April 2013)

Window Treatments with Style
Hannah Stanton
St Martin's Press (Spring 2015)

**Wood Finishing 101: The Step-by-
Step Guide**
Bob Flexner
Popular Woodworking Books (June
2011)

Young House Love
Sherry & John Petersik
Artisan (November 2012)

Opposite: Hand-embellished cabinet panels with a distressed, worn finish, GAP Interiors/Mark Bolton.

Websites and online resources

REFERENCE

Alabama Chanin
Natalie Chanin
Alabama, USA
www.alabamachanin.com
Hand-sewn clothing, home décor, and sewing workshops

Amy Butler Design
Ohio, USA
www.amybutlerdesign.com
Modern fabrics and sewing patterns

Annie Sloan
Oxford, UK
www.anniesloan.co.uk
Decorative painter, author, interior designer, developer of Chalk Paint®

Dan Clark
Colorado, USA
www.upscalewoodfinishing.com
Distressing how-to videos on YouTube

Janice Issitt Life Style
Janice Issitt
Buckinghamshire, UK
www.janiceissittlifestyle.blogspot.co.uk
Photographer, stylist, designer, blogger

Ki Nassauer
Minnesota, USA
www.kinassauer.com
Founder of Flea Market Style, Junk Bonanza, FleaQuest, and moderator of a wonderful online vintage-loving community

Knack Studios
Barb Blair
South Carolina, USA
www.knackstudios.com
Furniture studio, author, and designer

Meet Me at Mike's
Pip Lincolne
Melbourne, AU
www.meetmeatmikes.com
Design, craft & DIY blog and books

Miss Mustard Seed
Pennsylvania, USA
www.missmustardseed.com
Home décor blogger and author, creative force behind Miss Mustard Seed's Milk Paint

Perfectly Imperfect
Shaunna West
Alabama, USA
www.perfectlyimperfectblog.com
Painter, shopkeeper, budget-makeover maven

Royal Design Studio
California, USA
www.royaldesignstudio.com
Stenciling and decorative painting supplies, specialty brushes

Spruce Upholstery
Amanda Brown & the Sprucettes
Texas, USA
www.spruceaustin.com
Upholstery how-to workshops, upholstery tools, finished pieces, and accessories

Stencil Library
Northumberland, UK
www.stencil-library.com
Stencil supplier and inspiration blog

Wallovers
Connecticut, USA
www.wallovers.com
Stencils and specialty brushes

CONTRIBUTORS WEBSITES

551 East Design
Julia Miller
www.551Eastdesign.blogspot.com

Fawn Over Baby Blog
Melissa Hesseling
www.fawnoverbaby.com

Shades of Blue Interiors
Rachel Pereira
www.shadesofblueinteriors.com

Uptown Heirloom Company
Emily Skrehot & Philip Montanus
www.Etsy.com/shop/UptownHeirloomCo

Opposite: Chest of drawers with white stenciling by me & mrs. jones/ photograph by Stephanie Jones.

Case study biographies

MERIWEATHER ADAMS, My Kind of Refined,
www.mykindofrefined.com, Instagram: meriweatheradams
A Memphis, Tennessee native, Meriweather will soon graduate Auburn
University in Auburn, Alabama. Though she's only just recently picked up a
paintbrush and begun re-doing her thrift and yard-sale finds, she's already quite
proficient (and better yet, fearless) about tackling a furniture or wall makeover.
Being handy with a camera doesn't hurt, either. Though she's earned her degree
in Industrial and Systems Engineering she is looking forward to exploring
professional opportunities in the paint and design world as well. Meriweather
writes about her decorating and adventure in DIY on her beautiful blog, My
Kind of Refined. (Photo by Susan Waggoner)

CHRISTY BLACK, 11 Magnolia Lane,
www.11magnolialane.com, Facebook: 11 Magnolia Lane, Instagram:
11magnolialane, Twitter: @11magnolialane, Pinterest: Christy @ 11
Magnolia Lane
Christy Black is part of the dynamic trio that publish the popular blog 11
Magnolia Lane. Along with her friends Amy and Terry, Christy uses her creative
moxie to decorate stylishly on a conservative budget, inspiring their readers to
do the same. 11 Magnolia Lane is a made-up address, but these talented,
admittedly type-A ladies like their readers to feel as if they are hanging out with
them at home, chatting on topics ranging from re-doing furniture to remodeling
the kitchen to keeping the family organized…oh, and what's for dinner tonight.
Based all over the southeastern US, the 11 Magnolia Lane gang cover it all.
Christy uses her good sense, good humor, and great taste to transform the
plain-Jane into the fabulous. (Photo by Christy Black)

CLAIRE CHALKLEY, Les Couronnes Sauvages,
www.lescouronnessauvages.com, Facebook: Les Couronnes Sauvages,
Instagram: sauvages, Twitter: @couronnessauvage
A sought-after floral designer, Claire also excels at reviving furniture that to
other seems past its prime. Using wax, fabric, courage, and wit, she pulls off a
terrific look every time. Determined to lead a beautiful French revolution into
hers and others' homes using only "liberté, créativité, une tasse de thé," she is
an intrepd hunter of the flea market find, while blogging about flowers, France,
painted furniture, and rescued canines. Claire is a native Briton who makes
her home and keeps her shop in the lovely heart of Brittany.
(Photo by Claire Chalkley)

CHRIS GATCUM, IAmNotARobot,
www.iamnotarobot.co.uk, Facebook: Chris Gatcum
Author and award-winning photographer, Chris Gatcum, uses
his downtime to reinvent pieces of furniture and create one-off three-
dimensional art works under the pseudonym IAmNotARobot. A self-confessed
magpie, Chris has a workshop crammed full of found objects just waiting to be
reconfigured into new and unique creations. Rarely throwing anything away,
Chris is the perfect example of upstyler and recycler. (Image by Chris Gatcum)

KATE LANCEY-SMITH, Eats, Knits & Weaves,
www.eatsknitsandweaves.co.uk, Facebook: EatsKnitsWeaves,
Twitter: @eatsknitsweaves, Pinterest: eatsknitsweaves
Kate Lancey-Smith is the knits half of Eats, Knits & Weaves, a British company
making gorgeous things to eat and for the home. She is lucky enough to have
had a patient grandmother who taught her to knit as a child, and has been
doing it ever since. Kate is inspired by finding fresh twists for her knitting
projects: brightly knitted lampshades with sexy colored flexes; "Upknitted"
furniture (like upcycling but with wool) and making handknitted items, all with
something a bit different about them. Kate has sold at Spitalfields Market in
London and exhibited her work at the Brighton Artists Open Houses. (Photo by
Kate Lancey-Smith)

JOHNELLE MANCHA, Mignonne Décor,
www.mignonnedecor.com, Facebook: mignonnedecorshop, Instagram:
mignonnedecor, Twitter: @MignonneDecor, Pinterest: mignonnedecor
Johnelle studied in Paris, France, and Florence, Italy—both places figuring
importantly in the development of her style and references for her painted and
upholstered pieces. Her showroom in Berkeley features her team's creations,
and functions as a studio for Johnelle's work for clients in upholstery, repair,
custom-built furniture, color consultation, and interior design. The Mignonne
Décor team takes pride in sourcing vintage pieces, and using eco-friendly paints
for their projects. Johnelle visits France at least once a year to see her mother
and their sister shop The Bohemians, and to scout for treasures. (Photo by
Andrea Balazs)

NATALIA PRICE-CABRERA, Mols & Tati-Lois,
www.molsandtati-lois.com, Facebook: MolsTatiLois,
Twitter: @molsandtatilois, Pinterest: natipricecab
Natalia Price-Cabrera is the inspiration behind Mols & Tati-Lois, purveyor of
stunning boutique homewares and visual daily diarist. Fashioning beautiful
hand-tailored soft-sided and drum lampshades out of vintage and
contemporary designer fabrics using traditional techniques, Natalia creates
truly unique pieces. Her statement lampshades have been commissioned by
boutique retail outlets around the South East of England and as far afield as
Australia and the USA. Although lampshades are her main passion, Natalia
also upstyles furniture using paints and fabrics. (Photo by Chris Gatcum)

Glossary of terms

ALKYD
A base for paint or varnish that contains synthetic resins, most often oil-based.

APPLIQUÉ
A cut-out piece of fabric applied to another larger piece of fabric in a decorative manner.

BADGER
A very bushy but soft-bristled brush, used for softening or blending glazes between sections.

CAULK
A latex or rubber material used to fill in cracks, caulk comes in a tube and is used with a special applicator "gun." (Silicone caulk is excellent for plumbing applications, but is not paintable.)

DECK
Plain fabric, sometimes referred to as cambric, that covers the bottom of an upholstered piece.

DECOUPAGE
Meaning "to cut," a technique for creating a collaged effect on a surface—paper, fabric, and other two-dimensional materials are arranged and glued with a special medium.

DISTRESS
To age paint using an abrasive tool, such as sandpaper. This can also be marring a surface with a rock or hammer, or rubbing the paint back gently.

DRY-BRUSH
Painting with a barely loaded brush for a feathery-soft application or highlights.

DRY-EDGES
This happens when sections of a wash or glaze begin to harden before they are blended into the next area. Keep a wet-edge working!

FAUX BOIS
Literally "false wood," this technique creates wood grain in a glazed surface.

FLOGGER
A specialty brush with long, firm bristles used for dragging or strie techniques, and for wood-graining and faux bois effects.

FLY-SPECKING
A spatter of glaze, tinted shellac, or pigmented wax that gives the appearance of age.

FROTTAGE
Means "to rub," and is a way to give an ancient look to paint or plaster by applying a top layer thinly and then rubbing it or scraping it away.

GILDING SIZE
A special glue that dries to a barely tacky stage, allowing metal leaf to be applied. It may be water- or oil-based.

GILDING WAX
A soft wax containing metallic particles and pigments applied to give the effect of metal leaf.

GLAZE
A translucent medium used to extend the workable or "open" time of paint that allows texture to be created and makes paint more transparent.

GRAINING TOOL
Sometimes called a "rocker-grainer," this tool is used to comb through glaze and create the effect of wood grain and knots.

HEMP OIL
A lovely, light, food-quality oil derived from hempseeds, used to finish wood and paint.

LACQUER
A durable, glossy, high-end top coat that requires spraying. It is applied in several layers with sanding in between.

LAMINATE
A man-made material used in making furniture, often used as a top layer over less expensive materials such as chipboard.

LAP-MARKS
These are unattractive areas of double-coverage of a stain, wash, or glaze, easily prevented with a little care and blending.

LATEX/ACRYLIC PAINT
Water-based paints for walls, crafts, and furniture.

LEVELING

That beautiful, smooth look when the paint flows nicely and brushstrokes even out—characteristic of alkyd paints, lacquers, and enamels.

LIMING (OR CERUSING)

Gives a whitened or bleached look to paint or wood. A white wash or white-pigmented wax is now used to get the look of old wood that had been treated with a lime mixture to protect it from insects as was done years ago.

LINOLEUM BLOCK

Thick sheets of this artists' material are carved into shapes for stamping and printing.

METAL LEAF

Tissue-thin sheets of metal—typically silver, gold, and copper—that are adhered to a surface using size in a process known as gilding.

MILK PAINT

Casein-based paint that is liquefied with water before use. It is a traditional furniture paint that may also be used as a wash.

MYLAR

A clear, flexible plastic sheet used for creating stencils and templates.

NATURAL BRISTLE BRUSH

Made from boar's hair, natural or "China" bristle brushes range from inexpensive "chip" brushes to very fine artist's tools. They impart a little desirable texture to painted surfaces.

OFF-LOAD

Removing excess paint from the brush by swirling or pouncing onto a folded paper towel.

OMBRÉ

Meaning "to shade," an ombré effect is created with gradations of one color.

PATINA

The effects of age on a surface such as fading, oxidation, staining, wear and tear.

POLYURETHANE

In either water- or oil-based formulations, poly is basically a liquefied plastic that may be used as a top coat on wood or paint.

POUNCE

To apply paint or other coatings with a stippling or dabbing sort of brushstroke. A soft-bristled brush with a "flat" head works best for this technique.

PRIMER

An undercoat of paint that helps adherence and appearance.

PUDDLING

Occurs when a material such as stain or gilding size is applied too generously and pools of excess form, causing flaws in the finish.

REPEAT

One complete cycle of pattern in fabric, wallpaper, or stenciling.

REPOSITIONABLE ADHESIVE

A low-tack spray adhesive helpful when working with stencils or fabrics.

RESIST

A layer of wax, oil, or other material that will prevent paint from adhering. It creates a distressed and aged appearance.

SAGGING

Occurs when paint is over-applied to a vertical surface and pulls downward in "droopy," patchy areas.

SHELLAC

Created from the lac bug's secretion and denatured alcohol and/or ammonia, shellac dries to a hard, non-toxic finish and is used primarily over wood, but is also a terrific sealer for stains and under paint.

SOLVENT

A material that dissolves something else: mineral spirits, citrus solvent, and denatured alcohol are typical solvents used in painting projects.

STAIN

Available in lots of different colors and wood tones, stain is a penetrating, translucent finish for wood, but may be used as a glaze over paint.

STENCIL

A patterned mask created from mylar or oiled cardstock.

Glossary of terms continued

STENCIL
A patterned mask created from mylar or oiled cardstock.

STIPPLE
A pouncing brushstroke that creates a powdery application of paint.

STRIÉ
An effect achieved with a glaze or wash. A stiff-bristled brush is pulled through wet glaze or colorwash in one long, smooth stroke, creating soft lines. (Also known as "dragging.")

STRIPPER
A strong solvent used to dissolve and remove finishes such as paint and varnish from a surface.

SYNTHETIC BRISTLE BRUSH
Made of nylon or a similar synthetic material, these brushes create a smooth finish with water-based paints and coatings.

TACK CLOTH
Cheesecloth treated with a sticky substance so that wiping a surface will remove all dust and other debris.

TUNG OIL
Derived from the seed of the nut of the tung tree, an oil used as a durable finish for wood and paint, especially floors or exterior surfaces.

VARNISH
A clear-to-amber protective top coat, traditionally used over stained wood. Some varnishes also have UV light protection for exterior projects.

VENEER
A very thin layer of a finer wood (or other material) used on top of less expensive lumber in furniture making.

WASH
A thinned-down, translucent layer of paint.

WATER-SPOTTING
A technique when using a wash that creates a pattern of spatters.

WAX
An old-fashioned finish for wood or paint, clear or pigmented, that is worked onto a surface and then buffed to a sheen. It's made primarily from beeswax, carnauba, and/or other waxes.

WELTING
Fabric-covered cord that is used as a decorative trim on upholstery and also to reinforce the seams.

WET-DISTRESS
Working the edges back using a damp cloth or abrasive sponge on water-based paint.

Opposite: Desk with gilded edge by me & mrs. jones/photograph by Stephanie Jones.

Index

Index continued

Acknowledgments

Gratefuls go out far and wide to the many people who helped make this book a reality. First, thank you to the lovely group at Quarto and RotoVision who developed the concept and carried me through it: Isheeta Mustafi, Natalia Price-Cabrera, Tamsin Richardson, and their team—I've enjoyed our wonderful long-distance friendship. I owe huge thanks to Martha Hopkins at Terrace Partners, too.

My incredible and energetic team at me & mrs. jones has kept the studio and shop humming along during the process, as well as supporting the project with ideas, samples, and (most urgently!) cleanup. Jessica Bertel Mayhall, Cheryl Ott Westlake, Margaret Sheppard Apple, Renee Kent Lewis, Catherine Denton Wilfong, Kimberly King Bennett, Katherine Lang, and Elizabeth Humphreys Moore…I couldn't do anything without you all! Our "funterns" have been instrumental as well, especially Meredith Magness and my own Meg and Charlie.

Excellent teachers and mentors that have educated, inspired, and led me along the way also have their fingerprints all over this project. Immeasurable thanks go to Annie Sloan, Marian Parsons, Barbara Skivington, Helen Morris, Cynthia Davis, Natalie Chanin, Cindy Everett, Thomas Jayne, and John J. Tackett.

Many thanks to the talented and creative bloggers who were so willing to contribute their own work to the book: Meriweather Adams, Christy Black, Claire Chalkley, Chris Gatcum, Kate Lancey-Smith, Johnelle Mancha, and Natalia Price-Cabrera.

Most obviously, my family: my husband, Epps, and our children, Will, Charlie, and Meg. It goes without saying that the whole canoe doesn't stay afloat without you. And finally, thank you to my parents, Jan and Paul Johns, who have believed in me from the start.

Stephanie Jones